Advance Praise for The Four Speaking Energies

"Finally, a book that doesn't try to turn everyone into the same kind of speaker. Natasha gives you a framework to understand your natural strengths and expand them strategically. Practical, clarifying, and immediately useful."

- Aurora Winter, bestselling author of Turn Words Into Wealth

"Reading The Four Speaking Energies felt like holding up a mirror. When I came to the chapter on Water, I was struck by how accurately it captured the style I know to be my own—fluid, rhythmic, and adaptable. It not only affirmed my natural strengths as a speaker, but also challenged me to pause and consider new ways to harness and refine that power. Natasha's framework is both eye-opening and deeply practical for anyone who wants to own their unique speaking voice."

-Michelle Onuorah, bestselling author, public speaker & CEO of The Exit Lab

"Can you speak? Great. Now read Natasha's book. Do you see speakers that are larger-than-life and conclude: "That's the only way to speak"? WRONG. In The Four Speaking Energies, Natasha will show you how to identify your type of energy, and how to develop it with p.o.w.e.r. Do you wish to stay limited, or set yourself free?" - Daniel Alfon, LinkedIn strategist

"The Four Speaking Energies offers a fresh perspective on understanding and maximizing natural speaking strengths. By providing practical ways to develop and fine tune speaking energies, it is immediately applicable for helping Business English students hone their presentation skills."

-Debbie Nelson, EFL Business English instructor

"The Earth chapters, especially the example of Brené Brown blending grounded authority with warmth, left me feeling both confident and encouraged — a reminder that speaking with calm conviction and authenticity can inspire trust just as strongly as any fiery delivery." Sheldon S. Crocker, client and reader

"Wow! This wonderful book is the essence of developing a unique presence as a speaker. It is filled with proven applications for powerful public speaking, character development, and leadership. Highly recommended." - Terry Marsh, client and reader

"Natasha's book is fascinating and engaging. While reading I reflected on my own communication style, which evoked vivid memories and proved the validity of the test results." - Elena Poddashkina, client and reader

"Despite my many years of experience as an instructor, this book helped me look at my teaching style from a completely new angle and provided valuable insights aligned with my speaking energy - which I've just discovered through its pages." - Irina Safarova, client and reader

"Every word of Natasha's book was clear and understandable. When she described her fire energy I imagined her speech at once. Fascinating, loud, energizing, fast and full of emotions and laughter. The book is inspiring and full of beautifully described details."

Alyona Ozerova, client and reader

"Want to keep your audience's attention? Are you spending countless hours preparing your material, but your presentation is barely remembered? Then you simply need to read this wonderful book. You'll rethink your presentation style and gain the strength and confidence to deliver a successful public speech." - Julia Yermolayeva, client and reader

"This book is great opportunity to define, understand, and start to work on your way of speaking. At least entertain yourself by testing which speaking energy you have. Dig deeper into the book and Natasha will teach how to harness and leverage your energy if you want to ignite the audience."
- Iryna Malovichko, client and reader

THE FOUR SPEAKING ENERGIES

Unlock Your Natural Power as a Speaker

by

Natasha Bazilevych

Library of Congress Control Number (LCCN): 9781966647546

ISBNs:
eBook: 978-1-966647-53-9
Paperback: 978-1-966647-54-6
Hardback: 978-1-966647-55-3

Published by:
Authors Publishing House
178 Broadway, 3rd Floor, #1343
New York, NY 10001, USA

Main Line: (855) 624-0155
Email: support@authorspublishinghouse.com

.

Table of Contents

Dedication

To my Dad, who I believe is now with Jesus.

May this book honor his memory so that his name lives on.

About The Author

Natasha Bazilevych is a speaker and public speaking expert. She is Founder & President of Change View Academy, where she trains leaders to give powerful presentations.

Natasha holds a Bachelor's in Management of Organizations and an MBA. With nearly 20 years of experience, she has taught hundreds of students and clients globally.

In 2020, she was named one of the Top 500 Entrepreneurs by Brainz Magazine along with Simon Sinek, Mel Robbins and Jim Kwik. She has also been featured at Tony Robbins' and Dean Graziosi's World Summits (2021-2022), on ABC News in Duluth, MN, and various podcasts.

Acknowledgments

To my dear family and wonderful friends for always believing in me.

To my Mom for her love and never-ending persistent prayers.

To my brother Ruslan Bazilevych for editing my Speak With Power podcast for years and being a huge support for me.

To my best friends Nick and Maia Mikhaluk, Kevin and Debbie Nelson, and Annette Arnold for prayers, support, and inspiration.

To Brandon Cordon for designing the book cover, for encouragement, for his ideas, and insights.

To my business and speaking coach Michelle Onuorah for sharing her experience with me, for guidance and advice.

To my very first beta reader Daniel Alfon for taking the time to read the book when it was far from being ready, for his suggestions and help.

To Alex Sanfilippo, the creator of Podmatch, on whose platform I officially presented the idea for the first time.

To my very first business coach Dijana Llugolli for inspiration, guidance and having been the springboard for my speaking business.

To everyone who participated in the initial research, and those of you who cared enough to give me constructive feedback.

Introduction

Remember the last time you listened to a charismatic presenter and thought, "I wish I could speak like that"? What was your reasoning? Why can't you?

Is it because you're too nervous to speak to a crowd? Or do you think you don't have the same energy and charisma?

Since you've picked up this book, I'll bet there's something in you that's ready to get loud. Maybe you secretly dream of big stages or just want your ideas to be heard during company meetings.

Whatever it is, I'm here to tell you something important. Something about YOU: there's a chance you'll see yourself in a new way and will discover new opportunities for yourself.

......

It was the summer of 2002. I was a new member of a leadership team, standing before my colleagues, ready to begin training. At that moment, I felt like an imposter, doubting that anybody would take me seriously. I was so nervous that my mouth was dry, my limbs felt heavy, and my voice trembled when I first started speaking.

A million thoughts raced through my brain, hoping they wouldn't notice how shaky my voice was and trying to remember everything I planned to say. It's as if my mind went blank suddenly. I started feeling nauseous and all I could think of was – I want to be done with this as soon as possible.

It was more than 20 years ago. Since then, I've helped hundreds of clients and students from over 23 countries overcome their nervousness and speak with confidence. So, what helped me get to where I am now?

It took me two decades and thousands of dollars to master the art of public speaking and uncover my secret to becoming a powerful communicator.

I went from doubting my abilities to presenting with confidence and poise, from nervousness to calmness and clarity of mind, from feeling nauseous and hating public speaking to enjoying every moment of it.

I can't wait to share my secret with you.

....

You know what I've been hearing from people who come to my workshops and listen to my speeches?

"You have such amazing energy!" "Your energy is so incredible!"

And what do I answer them? YOU HAVE FANTASTIC ENERGY TOO!

You just need to understand it and start using it. We are all unique in our own ways and personalities. We all express ourselves in different ways. We perceive the world in unique ways.

So why do we think our speaking should be like everybody else's? Why do people look at Tony Robbins or someone else who is super energetic and think, "Well, this is how I want to speak."

If you are an introvert or a quiet person, it's not how you usually share thoughts. It's not natural for you. And you might have given up on the idea of speaking.

If you are an extrovert, you might have a lot of energy, like me, and sometimes think you need to channel it. Perhaps you're concerned that you're too emotional, loud, and overwhelming for others.

The thing is, most of us are too quick to criticize ourselves. We see our flaws much brighter than our advantages. We focus on our weaknesses more often than we appreciate our strengths.

In this book, I want to share with you something unique: four amazing speaking energies, four ways of expressing yourself, four styles of presenting. And one of them is you.

I would love for you to define your speaking energy and use it to express your uniqueness, brilliance, and superpower.

Look at your fingerprint - it's one of a kind. Look at your handwriting - it's only yours. Why then would you ever think that your speaking style, your speaking energy, should be someone else's? It could resemble another person. We might even adopt a few tricks and proven methods prominent speakers use to share their ideas. We'll continue growing and improving.

But our speaking DNA won't change. The core of who we are and how we express ourselves will stay the same.

So, let's dive into it. I have a practical and easy-to-follow 3D process. You'll DEFINE what your unique speaking style is, learn how you can DEVELOP it, and then DEMONSTRATE it to fulfill your mission on this earth.

Take the *Speaking Energy Self-Assessment* to discover your natural speaking style.

https://natashabazilevych.com/4speaking-energies-test

Part I

DEFINE

CHAPTER 1
Four Speaking Energies

"Today you are you, that is truer than true. There is no one alive who is you-er than you." - Dr. Seuss

"Slow down", "you're too hyper", "not so loud". I've heard these phrases too many times in my 20s. They made me think I need to be a different person. How can I work with adults, business owners, and CEOs if all they see is a hyper, overly enthusiastic girl?

To be honest, I even tried changing my personality. It didn't really work, but I sure tried. I kept telling myself, 'You've got to speak quieter, walk slower, and be calmer.'

What did help was my interest in the topic of Emotional Intelligence. I learned how to increase my self-awareness, manage my emotions, read others' feelings, and build relationships with them.

But I could never change who I am. At my core, I'm still that energetic, fast-moving, loud, and active girl whom I learned to embrace, accept, and understand. This girl is at her most beautiful when she unleashes all her passion, love, and fire, when she doesn't hold back and doesn't try to be someone else.

In my late 30s, I finally saw the beauty of being me. There's no need to copy someone else's style of speaking, moving, or living. There's harmony and peace in knowing your unique gifts and powers.

When I started teaching public speaking globally and heard the phrase "you have amazing energy" too many times, I knew there was something wrong with it. Being energetic and hyper doesn't mean having amazing energy. Knowing how to use your unique energy powerfully is what will make the difference.

And that's when I discovered four types of speaking energies, four ways we communicate with power in our unique way.

For the sake of simplicity and clarity, I'm using four elements to explain these four speaking energies: fire, water, air, and earth. Each of these elements generates a certain type of energy. Fire generates heat, water generates hydropower, air creates wind power, and earth produces bioenergy.

The same is true about our styles of speaking energy. Some people are on fire on stage. Others talk as if water is flowing. Then there are mysterious light speakers and finally, grounded, strong speakers with earth energy.

- Fire: Passionate, intense, fast

- Water: Flowing, emotional, balanced

- Air: Light, calm, intuitive

- Earth: Grounded, persuasive, steady

You don't need to become someone else. All you have to do is understand your speaking energy and leverage it to get the best results.

Are you FIRE like Tony Robbins, WATER like Barack Obama, AIR like Warren Buffett, or EARTH like Winston Churchill?

Let me tell you a story Warren Buffett shares about his speaking career.

When he was in high school and then college, he was absolutely terrified of public speaking. He avoided any classes that would require him to stand in front of other people and present. But he knew it was a necessary skill and decided to take the Dale Carnegie course.

Right after university, Warren volunteered to start teaching so he could practice his public speaking skills.

He knew he had to get out there and do it, so he forced himself into situations that would be uncomfortable and would require him to develop these new abilities.

When we hear Warren Buffett's speeches now, we can still see that timid teenager and hear the sign of his quiet, calm personality. At the same time, we hear confidence and strength in his voice and see passion and strength in his body language.

It's because he embraced who he was, found his voice, and developed his style. I would like to invite you to do the same.

We'll start with defining your style.

Let's look at each of these energies separately. You'll see how they're different from each other, and at the same time, how powerful each of these types is.

Of course, each one of us shares the qualities of all four archetypes. As we master our public speaking skills, we learn how to hone our abilities, harness our energy, and utilize the best features of all of them. However, there's always one type of energy we'll fall back to as a default.

When you read about each speaking energy, especially about those you don't consider your strong sides, pay attention to the attributes you'd like to develop. Make a list of features you think would help you become an even better speaker.

Summary:

Each of us carries a natural speaking energy — Fire, Water, Air, or Earth. The key to powerful communication isn't copying someone else's style but embracing and refining your own. Every energy has strengths and challenges, and by learning to recognize them, you can begin to speak with greater confidence and authenticity.

Well-Known Examples of the Four Speaking Energies

As you begin to explore the Four Speaking Energies, it helps to see how they show up in well-known individuals. Each of these speakers embraced their natural energy and used it to connect, inspire, and lead in their own unique way.

FIRE (Passionate, Intense, Fast)

- **Tony Robbins** – Commands the stage with high energy, intensity, and physical presence.
- **Gary Vaynerchuk** – Direct, blunt, rapid-fire delivery with raw passion.
- **Russell Brunson** – Persuasive, fast-paced style designed to excite and move people to action.
- **Grant Cardone** – Loud, high-intensity, driven — motivating through forceful passion.
- **Steve Jobs** – Dramatic and passionate, especially in product launches ("one more thing"), with bursts of intensity that captured global audiences.

WATER (Flowing, Emotional, Balanced)

- **Martin Luther King Jr.** – Rhythmic, emotional delivery that inspires hope and unity.
- **Simon Sinek** – Thoughtful, story-driven, appeals to deeper meaning and connection.
- **Lisa Nichols** – Vulnerable and powerful storytelling that flows with emotion.
- **Barack Obama** – Balanced cadence, inspiring yet measured, using pauses and flow effectively.
- **Maya Angelou** – Poetic, emotional cadence, deeply moving delivery.

- **Princess Diana** – Known for vulnerability and warmth, her speeches flowed with empathy.

AIR (Light, Calm, Intuitive)

- **Warren Buffett** – Conversational, calm, understated — quietly persuasive.
- **J.K. Rowling** – Reflective, thoughtful, often soft-spoken and imaginative.
- **Susan Cain** – Gentle, introvert-centered communication that draws people in.
- **Steven Spielberg** – Reflective and intuitive, often speaking with quiet vision.
- **Fred Rogers (Mr. Rogers)** – Soft, calm, deeply intuitive, creating space for connection.

EARTH (Grounded, Persuasive, Steady)

- **Winston Churchill** – Strong, resolute, steady delivery that grounded a nation in crisis.
- **Margaret Thatcher** – Firm, authoritative, unwavering presence — "The Iron Lady."
- **Oprah Winfrey** – Primarily Water in her empathetic style, but deeply Earth when teaching or guiding with authority.
- **Brené Brown** – Grounded in research and storytelling, steady and persuasive, with a calm authority.

- **Angela Merkel** – Calm, pragmatic, steady presence that reassured and persuaded through stability.
- **Nelson Mandela** – Grounded and firm, with a quiet authority that carried immense weight.

Reflection Questions:

1. When you think back on your own communication, what phrases or feedback have made you doubt your natural style?
2. Which of the four speaking energies feels most like your natural default, and why?
3. What qualities from the other energies would you like to intentionally develop?

Practical Tips

- **Observe Yourself as You Read:** Pay attention to moments in daily life where your natural energy shows up — in conversations, meetings, or even casual chats. Simply notice, without judgment.
- **Stay Open to Discovery:** As you read about each style, allow yourself to see possibilities in all of them. Don't rush to label yourself; instead, approach with curiosity.
- **Keep a Running List:** As you move through the next chapters, jot down words, phrases, or qualities that resonate. You may notice patterns that reveal your strongest energy.

CHAPTER 2

Fire

"The most powerful weapon on earth is the human soul on fire." —
Ferdinand Foch

This is my type, so it makes the most sense for me to start with it.

As you may know, fire generates thermal energy, which we refer to as heat. This thermal energy is created when a substance reaches its ignition point and reacts with oxygen. I won't go deep into physics now. All I want for you is to understand how this kind of energy is generated and what we can learn from it to understand our own speaking energy.

When was the last time you saw fire? Was it you lighting a candle, a gas stove, or making a bonfire in the backyard? As you may recall, it occurred because a type of fuel (wood, gas) underwent a chemical reaction with oxygen, and then it was heated to its ignition temperature.

Now, let's talk about what's happening with a speaker whose energy is Fire.

Just like fire can't be born in a place without oxygen, a speaker is not a speaker without an audience, even if those listeners are virtual. So, I would say that the main variable in the equation of any speaker, especially one with the FIRE archetype, is our care for the audience, our love for them, and our concern about their problems.

Add some passion about the topic, and you'll get a speaker on fire! That's the fuel that charges our speeches with high voltage. That's what creates the energy that shakes the ground and takes off ceilings.

Do you think your speaking energy is Fire? If it is, your pace is faster than usual. You're much more enthusiastic than most speakers. Your passion is sometimes over the roof.

You get so excited about the topic and so impatient to share it that you can barely control your own emotions.

Here are a few more features of speakers with FIRE energy.

They are fast and loud, confident and extremely passionate. Their body language is rich and expressive. They easily interact with the audience and have no problem speaking impromptu. Most FIRE speakers are extroverted and outgoing personalities.

There are a few areas where they need to be cautious.

They are fast thinkers and fast speakers. There's nothing wrong with it. But if you want people to understand you clearly and take action as a result of your speech or presentation, SLOW DOWN.

I'm preaching to myself here. It's been a remark I've heard from so many people whose energy is different from mine. They can't follow my pace, lose track of the points, and sometimes even lose interest.

Another danger for FIRE energy speakers is the risk of excessive enthusiasm and intense emotions. Again, there's nothing bad about being enthusiastic. It's actually our biggest power and advantage. But everything is good in moderation.

If your emotions overflow, if you can't control them at all, you risk overwhelming your listener, who will miss the main idea of the speech.

I recall a time when I was speaking with the leadership of my organization, sharing my ideas with them. And I got so excited and passionate that my emotions stood in the way of clearly explaining all the advantages of my ideas.

Suddenly, I saw confusion and loss of interest on their faces. "I've got to calm down", I told myself. I'm glad I read the audience soon enough to manage my energy and adapt it to the listeners. Eventually, understanding started to appear in their eyes, and their excitement finally matched mine.

So, when it comes to the other three speaking energies, it's essential to learn how to dial up their emotions and energy. For FIRE speakers, it's crucial to dial it down.

In the next part, we'll explore ways to manage our emotions, develop our speaking energy, and expand our style by learning from others.

Summary:

Fire speakers shine with passion, intensity, and speed. Their energy is contagious, igniting excitement and inspiring action. Yet their challenge is to balance enthusiasm with clarity, ensuring that their message doesn't get lost in the flames. When they learn to channel their fire with purpose, they can move audiences like few others.

Reflection Questions:

1. When you speak with others, do you notice yourself speeding up or raising your volume when passion takes over?

2. Can you recall a time when your enthusiasm either helped your message land with impact or made it harder for your audience to follow?

3. What signals (facial expressions, body language, or tone from your listeners) might help you notice when it's time to "dial it down"?

Practical Tips (for while you're reading this book)

- **Notice Your Triggers:** As you read, reflect on the topics that light your inner fire. When do you feel your energy rising quickly? Jot them down — they're clues to your natural fuel.

- **Watch for Audience Cues:** While going through the next chapters, practice imagining how different audiences might respond to Fire energy. Not everyone can run at your speed, and noticing that is part of mastery.

- **Balance Your Fire:** As you encounter Water, Air, and Earth styles in later chapters, consider which qualities could help balance your natural fire without dimming it.

Fire in Action: Well-Known Examples

Gary Vaynerchuk

Gary is the definition of Fire on stage and online. His delivery is fast, raw, and passionate, often overflowing with intensity. He doesn't polish his words — instead, he speaks straight from the gut. That unfiltered passion is what draws people in and makes him magnetic. But Gary also understands the need for balance. He has admitted in interviews that his intensity can sometimes be "too much" for certain audiences. Over the years, he's learned how to listen more, adjust his tone, and choose moments to unleash full energy. His ability to both ignite excitement and dial it back shows how Fire speakers can refine their style without losing their spark.

Steve Jobs

Jobs' product launches are some of the most iconic Fire moments in modern communication. With his famous "one more thing," he would hold an audience in suspense and then deliver with passion and intensity. His energy wasn't chaotic - it was controlled Fire, focused like a laser. That combination of drama, conviction, and excitement turned simple product reveals into cultural events. Yet Jobs wasn't always on full blast; in his Stanford commencement speech, he showed a quieter, more reflective side. Still, even then, the Fire was present - in his conviction, urgency, and emotional intensity. He's a powerful example of how Fire energy can be adapted to different settings while staying true to its essence.

CHAPTER 3
Water

"Nothing in the world is as soft and yielding as water. Yet for dissolving the hard and inflexible, nothing can surpass it."

— Lao Tzu

Now, let's dive into another speaking energy - WATER. This is perhaps the most balanced and adaptable of all the types.

I would like you to close your eyes and think of water. It could be a river, an ocean, a sea, a waterfall, or a brook in the woods. What features of water come to your mind?

Flowing, roaring, streaming, soft, strong. It's so diverse! It can be amazingly soothing and dangerously rough. Thanks to its flexibility, it's the most powerful speaking energy.

None of the other three elements can exist in three different forms: liquid, gas, and solid (ice). It shows how people with water speaking energy can be spontaneous, adaptable, and skilled at improvisation. They are also multifaceted. They adopt the qualities of other energies. They can be fast and roaring like fire, or mild and smooth like air.

There's one important thing to remember. Water can be still. Pour it into a glass, and it will simply sit there. But there's no energy. So how do we generate it? Let's look at hydropower. It's generated through the movement of molecules. Movement is the key here - movement of your body, movement of your voice.

If you want to harness water energy, you must learn how to manipulate your voice. Being monotonous is your death as a speaker. That's why you need to use vocal variety every time you speak.

Never use one pace and one volume of your voice. Speaking louder or quieter will make your speech more engaging and interesting, and will capture the audience's attention more effectively. Speed up or slow down based on the amount of emotion you want to convey and the meaning you assign to the content.

Play with rhythm. Get into the flow of your speech, then change the rhythm, and then change it again. Learn how to feel the flow, how to ride the wave. We will talk about developing your energy in Part II. For now, ensure that you can clearly define it.

If your speech sounds like a song, it's flowing, melodic, and rhythmic; there's a good chance that water is your primary speaking energy. If you are an introvert who knows how to leverage your confidence, it might be your style. If you're an extrovert who knows how to control your voice, you might have WATER energy.

Do you prefer to be spontaneous, or do you think it could become a strength if you develop it? Then you are a proud representative of this powerful speaking energy.

Do you remember Martin Luther King's "I Have a Dream" speech? If you've never heard it, definitely put it on your must-watch list. The way he projects his voice and influences crowds is a perfect combination of genuine emotion, passion, and conviction. At the same time, it's not hard or aggressive but flowing and smooth. He is in complete control of his vocal cords and all other articulation organs. He uses beautiful vocal variety and allows his tonality to create a speaking melody.

This is the ideal that we can all strive for. And yet, not everyone has this speaking energy. I said this before, and I'll repeat: don't try to be someone else, but learn from others to expand and develop your style of speaking.

Summary:

Water speakers bring rhythm, melody, and adaptability. Their power comes from flow, not force, and their ability to move with confidence while drawing listeners in emotionally.

Reflection Questions

1. When you think about your own communication, do you naturally create a sense of flow, or does your voice tend to become still like unmoving water?
2. How comfortable are you with vocal variety — changing your pace, tone, and rhythm as you speak?
3. Do you see adaptability and spontaneity as strengths in your speaking, or areas you'd like to develop further?

Practical Tips (for while you're reading)

- **Listen for Flow:** As you go through conversations or presentations in daily life, pay attention to the "melody" of your voice. Is it varied and flowing, or steady and flat?
- **Notice Flexibility:** As you read the next chapters, ask yourself how easily you can adapt — just as water changes shape based on its container. Do you hold steady, or shift naturally with your audience?
- **Collect Examples:** Each time you encounter a speaker (online, in person, or in media), jot down if they feel more flowing like Water, fiery like Fire, airy like Air, or grounded like Earth. This will sharpen your awareness of style.

Water in Action: Well-Known Examples

Martin Luther King Jr.

King's "I Have a Dream" speech remains one of the most powerful demonstrations of Water energy. His vocal variety, rhythm, and cadence create a flow that lifts and carries his audience. He balances conviction with smooth delivery, letting emotion wash over listeners without aggression. Even when speaking of urgent and painful truths, his voice was never harsh — it rose and fell like waves, blending passion with control. This balance of power and flow made his words not just heard, but *felt*, across generations.

Barack Obama

Obama embodies Water through his measured cadence and flowing sentences. He uses pauses intentionally, creating a sense of rhythm that keeps listeners engaged. His style is emotional yet controlled, inspiring hope without overwhelming. His speeches often carry a sense of inclusivity, inviting listeners to feel that they are part of a larger movement. He has the ability to build intensity gradually, like a river gaining momentum, carrying people along with him until the very end.

Maya Angelou

Maya Angelou's speaking style mirrors the cadence of her poetry. Her voice was rich, melodic, and deeply emotional, drawing listeners into a rhythm that felt like music. She channeled vulnerability and strength together, showing the softness and power of Water. In her recitations, every pause and every shift in tone carried weight, as though each word was rippling outward. She had the gift of making listeners not only understand her message but also experience its emotional resonance on a personal level.

CHAPTER 4

Air

"Air, I should explain, becomes wind when it is agitated." — Lucretius

It's time to discuss the most mysterious speaking energy - AIR. Let's remember everything we know about this element.

Air is light, invisible, free, always moving, seemingly weightless, and extremely powerful. It's constantly shifting, surrounding you. It's subtle, but it fills the space. It's calm, yet powerful, and its power is in its lightness.

But hey, let's stop for a little and question the perception of air weightlessness. Is it really true, or is it just our perception? We often see it as light and weightless. However, in fact, it has mass and occupies space. When air moves, it becomes unbelievably powerful.

Think of storms and tornadoes. The movement of air can carry heavy objects over long distances. It's capable of mass destruction and sometimes causes unthinkable disasters. So don't ever underestimate the power of air.

What does it say about people with AIR speaking energy? It suggests that they may be shy, or have been in the past, but their power lies in this very lightness, softness, and perceived weightlessness. They don't shout, demand attention, or take up a lot of space. But the more you listen, the more you feel drawn in. There's depth, clarity, and often mystery in the way they speak.

Don't mistake AIR speakers' gentleness with powerlessness. Unless they don't know how to use their voice and energy, these speakers obtain incredible strength and power.

Now, do YOU speak with AIR energy? Let's see. If you are an introvert with a quiet personality, there's a possibility that this is your speaking energy. If you feel there's subtlety and tenderness in your voice, elegance and softness in your manners, it's about you.

People with AIR speaking energy express themselves softly and gently. You'll never hear aggression in their voice. They are even a little mysterious and ethereal, beautifully elegant and perfectly agile.

They are naturally intuitive. They sense the emotional undercurrents in the room and read between the lines. They choose their words carefully and often say less, but mean more.

This can be a powerful tool in public speaking, especially in a noisy world. When everyone else is competing for attention, the AIR speaker draws attention through contrast. Their stillness becomes magnetic.

It brings us to the question of how wind power is generated. Just like hydro power, it requires the movement of molecules. There's no energy in still air. That's why, for every speaker with AIR energy, it's essential to develop their voice and learn how to use their power.

Many representatives of this archetype lack confidence in themselves because they are unaware of their strengths and incredible possibilities.

One of my amazing clients speaks with this fantastic style. He has a calm personality and was once shy. However, he worked on himself extensively and developed a great deal of confidence, which led him to start teaching others how to do the same.

Before we worked together, he thought the only way to be a prominent speaker was to have over-the-top energy, a loud voice, lots of movements, and act like Tony Robbins on stage. Now he knows his speaking energy is as valuable. It's unique, powerful, and connects with people on a deeper level.

We will discuss the development of this speaking energy further in Part II. You'll know how to see your power and harness it. You'll understand what attributes of other energies can help you become a fantastic presenter and always speak with poise.

For now, remember this: if you are an AIR speaker, own it. Your calmness is your strength, and your stillness can be powerful. You don't need to become anyone else - just step fully into yourself, with intention.

AIR isn't about performance; it's about presence.

Summary:

Air speakers influence not through noise, but through presence. Their calmness, clarity, and subtlety invite audiences in, creating deep connection. In a world that often equates loudness with power, Air reminds us that sometimes the quietest voice carries the furthest.

Reflection Questions

1. Do you tend to underestimate your own voice or presence because it's not loud or forceful?
2. Have you ever experienced a moment when quietness or calm made people lean in more to listen?
3. What role does intuition play in how you communicate with others?

Practical Tips (while you're reading)

- **Notice Stillness:** As you continue this book, observe how pauses, silence, or quiet tones can sometimes hold more weight than words.
- **Listen Differently:** The next time you hear someone speak softly or slowly, resist the urge to compare them to louder speakers. Instead, ask yourself how their presence draws you in.
- **Track Subtle Strengths:** Keep a small list of moments when you or others influenced people without raising volume or intensity. This will remind you that calmness can be magnetic.

Air in Action: Well-Known Examples

Susan Cain

Author of *Quiet*, Susan Cain brought global attention to the strengths of introverts. Her TED Talk has been viewed over 40 million times - not because she spoke loudly or dramatically, but because she spoke truthfully, gently, and with presence. Her message floated in quietly, yet stayed with audiences long after. Cain's choice to highlight vulnerability and reflection made her message even stronger. She showed that you don't need volume to have impact - authenticity and calm conviction can be just as persuasive, if not more.

Fred Rogers (Mr. Rogers)

Rogers is a masterclass in Air energy. With his quiet demeanor, soft pacing, and gentle tone, he created trust with millions of children and adults. He proved that you don't need to shout to be heard — safety and authenticity can be far more powerful than volume. His stillness was not weakness; it was his strength. Rogers also modeled patience, often using silence intentionally, giving children the time and space to think and respond. In a world of noise and rush, his calm presence became a refuge and a powerful example of leadership through gentleness.

Warren Buffett

Buffett is one of the most successful investors in history, yet his speaking style is humble and conversational. He doesn't rely on big stage tricks - instead, he explains complex financial ideas with simplicity and calm. His steady presence makes him approachable, even when speaking to thousands. Buffett's annual shareholder meetings are legendary not because of flashy delivery but because of his clarity, humility, and the sense of reassurance he gives. He demonstrates how quiet confidence and straightforward honesty can build immense credibility and trust - the essence of Air energy in leadership.

CHAPTER 5
Earth

"Look deep into nature, and then you will understand everything better."
— *Albert Einstein*

And finally, the most confident type of speaking energy is EARTH. Each archetype is powerful, but this one has a unique expression. When you listen to a speaker with this energy, the first description that comes to mind is one of being grounded, solid, and persuasive.

You would feel a sense of stability and even a sense of weight in the way these speakers exude their energy. They love to use dramatic pauses. They pace themselves and never hurry. They speak with such conviction that nobody would dare doubt them.

You can hear a rhythmic flow of sounds, perfect diction, and an inevitable impression of power. EARTH speakers who take the effort to develop their speaking energy possess unquestionable executive presence. Whether male or female, they often talk with a low-pitched voice, rich timbre, and falling inflection.

These speakers always pace themselves and are never in a hurry. They don't need to be flashy or expressive. They don't push or overact. Their power lies in showing up with weight and wisdom.

If you have a calm and deeply confident personality, and you've mastered the art of persuasion, chances are you speak with EARTH energy.

You might recognize an EARTH speaker by these traits:

- Speaks with calm, steady pacing

- Uses fewer words, but makes them count

- Rarely overuses gestures - every movement has purpose

- Often introverted or internally focused

- Leads with logic, structure, and grounded presence

This energy is incredibly powerful—especially in high-stakes settings such as boardrooms, negotiations, or crisis communications. People look to EARTH speakers for stability.

Winston Churchill is the best representative of this speaking energy. When you hear him speak, every word carries weight. It's as if each one drops with gravity and intention. He exudes power. He may be a little monotonous, but the perfect rhythm of his speech synchronizes everything into one marching sound. His words were not flashy, but they were monumental. "We shall never surrender." That's EARTH energy.

To understand this energy even better, let's take a brief look at how biopower is generated.

Biomass fuels are converted into heat and electricity through burning, decomposition, or conversion into gas or liquid fuel. This metaphor illustrates how Earth and Fire energies may appear similar but function in distinctly different ways.

In both types heat is generated through burning. It's a rather fast and powerful process. However, biopower can also be generated through decomposition, a process that takes considerable time.

Speakers with both energies exude extreme confidence but their pace and level of excitement is different. FIRE speakers are fast and enthusiastic. EARTH speakers are calm, grounded and never in a hurry.

One of the greatest strengths of EARTH speakers is their reliability. But this can also become their greatest weakness. Their steady presence can sometimes feel rigid, overly serious, or emotionally distant. That's why it's important for EARTH speakers to soften at times - make eye contact, tell a story, smile, show some warmth. Your audience wants to feel your humanity as well as your strength.

Summary:

Earth speakers communicate with gravity, steadiness, and authority. Their words carry weight, their presence inspires trust, and their calmness provides stability. When softened with warmth, Earth energy becomes not only powerful but unforgettable.

Reflection Questions

1. When you speak, do people often describe you as calm, steady, or persuasive?

2. How comfortable are you with silence and pauses when you communicate?

3. Do you sometimes worry about coming across as too serious or distant? How might you show warmth without losing your grounding?

Practical Tips (while you're reading)

- **Notice Stability:** As you read the next sections, pay attention to moments when a steady voice or calm presence makes communication more effective.

- **Lean Into Pauses:** Experiment with the idea of pausing in conversations or presentations — notice how silence can create gravity and invite attention.

- **Balance with Warmth:** As you reflect on Earth energy, jot down small ways you can add warmth — a smile, a personal story, or more eye contact — to balance authority with approachability.

Earth in Action: Well-Known Examples

Margaret Thatcher

Nicknamed "The Iron Lady," Thatcher's speaking style reflected the firmness and authority of Earth energy. Her low, steady voice and precise diction conveyed strength and resolve. She rarely rushed, allowing each point to land with force. Thatcher projected control and confidence even under fierce criticism. While some perceived her as rigid, her steadiness gave her authority and made her a global symbol of resolve. She is a clear example of how Earth speakers can anchor a message in strength and conviction.

Angela Merkel

Merkel is a modern representation of Earth energy in leadership. Her communication style is calm, pragmatic, and deliberate. She avoids theatrics, instead relying on logic, structure, and grounded presence. During moments of crisis, such as the Eurozone financial turmoil or the refugee crisis, Merkel's steady voice reassured citizens and colleagues alike. Though she is understated, her ability to project stability and quiet authority made her one of the most respected leaders in the world. Merkel shows that Earth power doesn't need to be loud — it is persuasive precisely because it is unshakable.

Brené Brown

Brown brings a more personal and accessible expression of Earth energy. Her speaking style is steady and grounded, but she layers it with warmth and vulnerability. By combining research with relatable storytelling, she commands attention without theatrics. Her TED Talk on vulnerability became one of the most viewed talks in the world not because of flashy delivery but because of her authenticity and authority. Brown demonstrates that Earth energy can persuade through both credibility and humanity, showing that groundedness and warmth together create lasting impact.

CHAPTER 6
Summary of 4 Types

"The privilege of a lifetime is to become who you truly are." - C.G. Jung

A lot of speakers try to mimic a certain type and unfortunately end up sounding fake and, in some cases, even ridiculous. If it's not a part of your nature, don't try to pretend like this is your speaking energy. Don't copy someone else. Find your own style. That's what this book is all about.

You are unique! And your speaking energy may differ from that of your favorite speakers. Embrace who you are and be the best version of you. This way you will bring the most value to the world around you.

The most fascinating fact about all four types of speaking energy is that they are all connected. Each one of them is unique but they share certain qualities. It makes them multifaceted, and agile.

Let's look at this diagram of all four types and what qualities they have in common.

As you can see, the types that are next to each other share common qualities. Both FIRE and WATER are fast talkers, enthusiastic and emotional. Depending on the level of development of their speaking energy and their personality, some speakers are more animated and vivacious than others.

Yet, there's a clear difference between FIRE and WATER speakers. Speakers with WATER energy are softer, more melodic, and flowing; speakers with FIRE energy are more abrupt, sharp, and a bit rough.

They share these qualities with EARTH, as well as confidence in speech and enunciation of words. However, don't think that only FIRE and EARTH speakers are confident personalities. Not at all. All four speaking energies can convey confidence, but those two do it with more emphasis and definiteness, as if there can be no doubt about what they are saying.

Let's examine the energies of water and air. They are both soft and flowing, gentle and elegant. However, WATER speakers usually talk faster and louder, with more melody. At the same time, AIR speakers express themselves more softly and lightly, as if floating in the sky.

And at the same time, there are similarities between AIR and EARTH speakers. Even though they seem so different, both these speaking energies are not in a hurry. These speakers like to pace themselves well, and pauses are their good friends.

The striking difference between them is the heaviness of EARTH speakers and the lightness of AIR presenters. While speakers with EARTH energy are grounded, speakers with AIR energy appear weightless.

As you can see, all four speaking energies are interconnected. That's why you might question your type sometimes if the qualities of another speaking energy fit your style.

However, your way of speaking is unique. Define it, understand it, and work on it. None of the four speaking energies is better than the other. They are all powerful, impactful, and strong if you develop them.

As soon as you become comfortable in your skin, with your own speaking energy, you'll know how to show your best qualities, amplify your strengths, and neutralize your weaknesses. You'll not only develop your speaking energy, but you will start expanding it, stretching yourself, tapping into other energies, and using them depending on the situation.

When I was younger, my impulsiveness and high energy were the only way I could operate. I didn't possess enough emotional intelligence skills to manage my emotions. I recall how, in my early twenties, I collaborated with a world-renowned business trainer on a workshop for a major national insurance company. It was an exciting opportunity, and my emotions were flying high. I had no idea how to act cool and calm in front of C-suite executives. When I first met the company's President, his attitude towards me was extremely skeptical. It took me a couple of days to demonstrate my professionalism and the benefits of my passionate nature in changing his attitude.

By the end of the three-day training, he expressed enormous gratitude and respect to me, which was an encouragement and inspiration for me to continue developing my skills and refining my own style.

So that's what we'll be talking about in Part II of this book.

You'll learn how to increase the power of your speaking energy so that your speeches and presentations are clear, persuasive, and inspire action.

Summary:

The four speaking energies are distinct, but interconnected. Each carries unique strengths and challenges, and each becomes powerful when embraced authentically. Your task is not to imitate, but to uncover and refine your own energy. As you move into the next part of this book, you'll learn how to strengthen your style, expand your range, and speak with clarity, confidence, and impact.

Reflection Questions

1. Which of the four energies felt most familiar as you read the first part of this book?
2. Did you recognize qualities from another energy that you'd like to strengthen in yourself?
3. How might embracing your authentic style instead of copying someone else's change the way you speak and connect with others?

Practical Tips (while you move into Part II)

- **Keep a Journal of Insights:** As you read Part II, jot down one strength and one growth area you notice in your own style for each chapter.
- **Stay Open to Blending:** Even if you identify strongly with one energy, stay curious about others. You may find new tools that enrich your natural style.
- **Revisit the Diagram:** Glance back at the chart of all four energies from time to time. It's a reminder that your style exists within a spectrum, not a box.

Part II
DEVELOP

CHAPTER 7

Speaking And Running

"Running is the greatest metaphor for life because you get out of it what you put into it." — *Oprah Winfrey*

There were many mornings when I knew I needed to go for a run because I had trained for a race and needed to put in miles, but it was unbelievably hard to drag myself out of bed.

I remember one day I heard the alarm, changed it to go off 5 minutes later, and 10 minutes later, and went back to sleep. Then, when it rang both times, I would think of every excuse not to get up (I need rest, maybe I'll run tomorrow). But I knew there wouldn't be another chance. So, I forced myself out of bed. It was hard to take that first action, but as soon as I did, the rest was much easier.

I got outside, ran a few miles, and guess what thoughts were going through my mind on my way back home – I did it! It feels amazing! I feel like a superhero; I think I can do anything now.

That's what happens when we take action. It's hard to make the first step, but as soon as we do, the reward is so worth it.

Defining your speaking energy is not enough. As soon as you know and understand your style, it's time to take action, work on developing it, expanding, and growing it.

...

Now that we have looked at all four types of speaking energy and you have defined yours, let's talk about the DEVELOP stage.

There's no point in defining and understanding your type if you are not going to do anything about it. So, let's roll up our sleeves and start working on our speaking energy so that we can deliver the presentation powerfully.

However, there's one word I'd like to introduce to you first. Commitment.

Unless you commit to the process of development, there will be no growth, and you'll never know how high you could fly.

If you've ever trained for a marathon, you know - crossing the finish line is the best, one of the most powerful moments we can experience. But you can't have that without spending four months in training. You develop your energy, your speed, your muscles. You work on your form and your endurance.

It takes time. And it takes COMMITMENT.

Have I told you I'm a runner? Yep! A marathoner, actually. I ran seven marathons and 11 half-marathons.

Not long ago, I discovered that being a runner and a speaker complement each other well. These two activities unexpectedly complement each other. Who would have thought?

There are so many commonalities. The importance of training is just one of them. Before we dive into each type separately, let's discuss the general advice for developing your speaking energy. We will examine it from the perspective of a marathoner.

.....

Breathing

All speakers, as well as runners, need to understand the importance of correct breathing. If we don't develop sufficient capacity in our lungs, we won't be able to speak with a powerful, strong, and persuasive voice. Just as a runner needs lungs for speed, strength, and endurance, speakers use their lungs for volume, power, and vocal variety.

Let me tell you about my first-ever race, and you'll understand the importance of working on your breathing and developing your lung capacity.

It was the year 2012. I had just started running more regularly because my boyfriend at the time challenged me to run a marathon in October of that year. But as we all know, big goals are achieved by taking smaller steps. So I started with a 10K race in April.

Three of my friends and I arrived at the main square in Kyiv with high expectations, nervous anticipation, and a sense of excitement. Several of us were about to experience a race for the first time in our lives. I don't remember who suggested running a small race first to see what it's all about.

But I'm eternally grateful to that person because it was definitely not what I expected.

When the anthem ended and the gun was shot, we all started running. It was initially easy and exciting. Lots of runners around you, music is playing, adrenaline is pumping. But the excitement didn't last long. After a few hills and the cobblestone parts of the course, exhaustion started kicking in. My breath became short and shallow. I couldn't inhale deeply and felt like I was dying.

I'll remember that moment for the rest of my life. It was not far from Saint Sophia's square in Kyiv, and the finish was close. But I couldn't make myself go further. All I could think about was I want to stop running, lie down right here, and die.

Of course, I didn't. I breathed in, pulled myself together, and kept going. My finish time wasn't the best, but it was still a great accomplishment. I ran my first race!

When you give your first speech or presentation, you might also feel out of breath. Whether that's nervousness, fear, or something else, always remember to breathe deep and keep going no matter what.

Here's my favorite proven breathing technique.

Breathe in slowly, hold your breath for three seconds, and then slowly exhale. Works like a charm. Once this technique slowed my breathing so much that I almost failed my heart test for marathon runners.

It was five or six years ago. Before running a half-marathon, I needed to obtain a medical certificate confirming that my health was sufficient to participate in the event. One of the tests was an electrocardiogram. It was early in the morning, and I was hurrying to the doctor's office. When I finally arrived, my heart rate was racing, so I needed to slow it down. I risked being denied the certificate. So I breathed in slowly while sitting in the waiting room. I counted to three and slowly breathed out. After doing it a few times, my heart rate slowed down so much that a part of the diagram on the doctor's monitor was almost flat. She looked at me with curiosity but still issued a certificate.

See? You can calm yourself using breathing techniques. You can learn to manage your breath and strengthen your lungs. And then both running and speaking would be more effective, and with great results.

Importance of Training and Practice

Have you ever attempted to run a marathon without training for several months? I haven't, but some people have.

An acquaintance once told me that he decided to run a race without doing any training runs. He started strong, full of adrenaline like all of us at the START line. When you hear the music, the anthem, and the sound of a gun, and start running together with thousands of others, the feeling of excitement carries you forward for about 3-4 miles. After that, it becomes increasingly difficult.

When he was coming closer to the finish line, he couldn't feel his legs. The speed was slow, and the mindset was weak. He thought he was going to die. The next day, he couldn't get up from his bed. And the next few days, he could barely walk.

Practicing and training before a big race is as important as learning public speaking techniques and rehearsing your speech before a big event.

I usually train for 12-16 weeks for a half-marathon and 18-20 weeks for a full marathon. It's crucial to prepare your mind, heart, lungs, and legs for those long 13 or 26 miles (that's 21 or 42 km).

And imagine if you don't prepare your speech and don't practice it, but decide to wing it completely. It would be a disaster. Even if you can speak impromptu perfectly well, it's disrespectful to your audience to spend no time in preparation for your presentation. Unless, of course, you're not given any time for that and you're invited to speak on the spot.

So, make sure you put in enough hours into your preparation: research your audience, choose the best opening to grab their attention from the start, include personal stories, and finally, end it with a memorable closing.

Mindset is Everything

Everything starts with mindset. It's true about more than just speaking and running. It's true in business, money, relationships, and personal growth.

When I first start working with my clients, we always begin with a mindset. Before you even start writing your speech or presentation, it's crucial to look inside, dig deep, and understand yourself. What motive do you have for this speech? Why do you want to share this message?

Do you have any fear of public speaking? What is the root of it?

Often, people experience stage fright, which stems from their fear of failure, judgment, and rejection. And that's what we initially need to work on.

If you don't have a fear of public speaking, and you don't even get nervous before a speech, you are a rare breed. I must admit that I get a bit anxious if the audience or message is new. That's absolutely normal. And handling such situations is what mindset work is all about.

What you've got to do is build confidence. Everyone suffers from imposter syndrome. Ok, not everyone. Only those who are brave enough to get out of their comfort zone and try something new. That's when self-doubt and imposter syndrome will kick in.

So, what do we need to do to build confidence? Prepare and rehearse, visualize and believe.

Let's examine the process of developing the right mindset for running a marathon.

If your mind is not trained, no amount of miles your legs have run would prepare you for what's to come. The mind needs to be strong and ready to persevere through the moment of hitting a wall, typically around mile 20.

How do we work on that? Practicing, training, visualizing, believing. A few years ago, I read a book by an Olympic runner. She was sharing her process of preparing for a marathon. One moment in particular stood out to me.

You know how many people consider visualization something intangible, woo-woo, and weird? I was one of those people. Until I found out it's a legitimate technique used by professional athletes.

First, you have to visualize your success, and then it becomes a reality. It's exactly what that Olympic runner was doing with a coach. He would have her lie down on the floor, close her eyes, and see the whole race in her mind. She wouldn't just visualize the finish, but all stages, especially the hard moments. She would see herself overcoming those obstacles, pushing through the pain, and finishing strong.

That's what I do in speaking as well. Before each significant speech or presentation, I would visualize myself giving it. I would see my audience responding, prepare myself for difficult questions, imagine challenging moments, and see myself overcome them. In 99% of cases, it happens exactly how I visualize it.

Let's review what we just talked about. Mindset! Everything starts with it. First, build strong beliefs in your abilities, visualize your success, and work on your confidence. And that's what will bring you success in speaking as well as running races.

…………

These are the main similarities between speaking and running races.

Here are a few more:

- Affirmations and mantras work like magic
- It's exciting and scary at the same time
- You've got to get out of your comfort zone
- Hiring a coach will advance your skills.

And that's not all. Let's see what other people think about it.

One of my best friends, Debbie Nelson, who ran 18 full and 32 half marathons, said about both running and speaking: "Consistent practice and discipline pay off over the long haul!"

Terry Marsh, a dear friend and client, said: "It can raise your standards, reset your beliefs. It helps to develop grit and determination for the long game. Many small steps forward, taken with determination, add up to the distance run. Many well-chosen words delivered with impact and passion mean a speech well done."

A seasoned triathlete, marathoner, and successful business owner, Shavkat Musinov recommends: "Be in the moment here and now, accept the whole real situation as it is, enjoy the process."

A podcaster, Amanda Marie Acker, wisely noted:

"I am not a public speaking pro, but I love this comparison. I ran part of a marathon, and it took a lot of training and positive affirmations to cross the finish line. The same applies to speaking. I was scared of running that marathon, but I did it, and I know I can nail public speaking too with practice, help, and reminding myself that I got this and can cross the finish line!"

Summary: Speaking and Running

Developing your speaking energy is like training for a marathon. At first, the hardest part is simply showing up - taking the first step, committing to the process, and pushing past the excuses. Just as runners train their lungs, legs, and mindset, speakers must train their breath, body, and confidence.

Breathing fuels your presence, training and practice sharpen your skills, and mindset carries you through the hardest moments. Visualization, preparation, and consistency transform fear into focus and self-doubt into determination.

Both running and speaking demand commitment. There are no shortcuts - only steady effort, daily discipline, and the willingness to step outside your comfort zone. And just as crossing the finish line brings exhilaration, so does delivering a powerful speech. The reward is not just in the moment itself but in knowing you grew stronger with every mile and every word along the way.

Reflection Questions

1. When you think about your speaking journey, what "first step" feels hardest to take right now?
2. How do you usually prepare for a high-stakes presentation, and how does that compare to how you'd train for a race?
3. What fears or doubts show up before you speak, and how might visualization or mindset practices help you overcome them?
4. Which lesson from running - breathing, training, or commitment - feels most relevant to your growth as a speaker today?

Practical Tips

- **Start Small but Consistent:** Just like a runner doesn't begin with 26 miles, begin with short, regular speaking practice. Record yourself for 2–3 minutes daily to build stamina and confidence.

- **Use Breathing as a Tool:** Before your next presentation, practice the "inhale–hold–exhale" technique to calm nerves and strengthen vocal power.

- **Visualize the Finish Line:** Before stepping on stage, take five minutes to picture yourself delivering with clarity and impact, handling challenges with confidence, and leaving your audience inspired.

- **Commit Publicly:** Sign up for a speaking opportunity - at work, church, or a local group. Like registering for a marathon, the commitment will hold you accountable to train and prepare.

CHAPTER 8
Develop Fire

"Be still when you have nothing to say; when genuine passion moves you, say what you've got to say, and say it hot." — D.H. Lawrence

Let's look at each speaking energy separately. How can we develop our energy? Each one of them is unique and requires a specific set of techniques and methodologies.

After defining your energy, it's crucial to accept it. Don't try to be someone else. Don't think that one of them is better than the other. They are all equally powerful!

I'll tell you the truth. When I was younger, probably in my 20s and 30s, I wanted to be calmer and less energetic. I thought it was more impactful to walk and talk slowly.

I don't think that way anymore. I accepted my energy. I know I'll be the same Natasha in my 50s and 60s. Still enthusiastic, sometimes hyper, rarely completely calm. And it's beautiful. It doesn't make me less powerful than others.

However, if we want to grow professionally as speakers, it's important to develop certain aspects of our speaking energy. For example, as a representative of FIRE energy, I needed to learn how to harness my energy and use my enthusiasm. It's essential to convey my passion without letting it become too loud and overshadow the message's meaning.

How do we do that?

First, master breathing techniques. We have already discussed them in previous chapters. But let me tell you how I calm my nerves and manage my emotions right before the presentations.

It was one of my first speech competitions. I was sitting in a room full of other participants waiting for my turn to speak. My palms were sweaty, my heart was pounding, and I could hear blood rushing to my temples.

No way would I deliver a powerful speech in such a condition. I knew I'd be nervous and unable to control my energy. My enthusiasm would break the charts, the pace would be too fast, and the delivery too weak.

So, about 5 minutes before it was my turn, I relaxed in my chair and closed my eyes. "Time to breathe", - I told myself. I inhaled deeply, held my breath for 3 seconds, and exhaled slowly.

Just like I told you before. Works like magic - every time.

After calming my nerves, it was time to expend some energy. I got up from my chair, walked out of the room, and moved my body a bit.

What's interesting is that moving your body (jumping jacks, little exercise, a bit of dancing) helps both in the case of too high or too low energy. We'll address that in future chapters.

Let's get back to my story. It's almost time for me to speak. I walk back into the room with all the listeners, judges, and other participants. I come to the front, look at everybody with a smile, and pause.

Don't start speaking right away. Take a moment to gather your thoughts. Give your listeners a chance to prepare their minds for another message.

This pause, smile, and confident look into the audience are great techniques for managing your emotions and energy. It's a powerful move.

As you remember, FIRE energy speakers tend to speed up and neglect pauses. But if you start with a pause, it will set the tone for the whole speech.

Now, what have we established so far? To develop your FIRE energy,

1. Use breathing techniques to calm your nerves.
2. Release your energy through body movements to get rid of some extra energy and bring it to a normal, manageable level.
3. Pause before your speech, look at the audience with a confident smile, and start speaking.

Fire energy can be a destructive force if it is not controlled. That's why it's important to develop it like any other skill.

First, find ways to practice it, and every time you get to speak, pay attention to your pace. Learn to control your energy. Imagine that you have a superpower and you can't just unleash it because it will sweep everything off. You've got to be in charge and take control.

Like in running, when I start a marathon, there's so much excitement and energy that I naturally speed up. Every time I tell myself to start slow and hold back to preserve my strength for the middle of the race. But every time I hear the music and people cheering, my adrenaline gets out of control, and I start running faster without realizing it.

The result, of course, is exhaustion after a few such intense miles.

That's why it's important to control our excitement both in running and speaking. And mind you, I'm talking specifically about those of us who have FIRE speaking energy, who are naturally enthusiastic. About a lot of things. Who easily gets excited.

Other types would have no problem controlling their excitement. They might actually need to dial it up a little.

Another important skill for FIRE speakers is to harness our nervous energy and extreme excitement, and turn it into passion. Every speaker needs to show love for the topic. For us, it shouldn't be a problem. However, too much enthusiasm could become an obstacle. It risks overshadowing the message. If emotions are too loud, your enthusiasm will overwhelm the audience, and the listener won't hear the main point.

So, how do we transform our nervous energy into passion while also maintaining control? Learn to channel your nervousness, direct it to your message, and then focus completely on your audience.

For that, it's important to shift the focus from you to your listener. As soon as you start thinking about the problem you're solving for them, your fears dim and then disappear.

And if you still feel a little nervous, say to yourself: I'm not anxious, I'm just excited. I've done it hundreds of times before presentations, speeches, contests, and super-important interviews.

Repeat it a few times if you need. Visualize your nervous energy as a funnel, change its color, and transform it into captivating passion and enthusiasm. This kind of imagination technique will help you manage your nervousness and utilize it to your advantage.

There's one more thing I will say to all of you, fellow FIRE speakers. Choose your preferred method of exercise and make it a habit. Whether it's running, cycling, playing sports, dancing, swimming, or anything else.

With our crazy energy, it's crucial to find ways to express it. That will help you remain more in control of your emotions when presenting.

Plus, the endorphins your body generates during a workout will help boost your confidence and positive mindset, which is so much needed for every speaker.

Summary: Developing Fire

FIRE energy is powerful, passionate, and contagious, but it can also burn out of control if left unmanaged. The key for Fire speakers is balance: learning to calm nerves, release excess energy, pause with intention, and transform nervousness into passion. By shifting focus from self to audience, controlling pace, and finding healthy outlets for excess energy, Fire speakers can deliver with both intensity and clarity. When passion is channeled, Fire becomes not overwhelming, but magnetic.

Develop your FIRE energy using the following techniques.

1. Breathing techniques to calm your nervous system.
2. Move your body (dance, light exercise, jumping jacks) to release your energy and bring it to a manageable level.
3. Practice pausing before your speech to collect your thoughts and start the presentation with confidence and poise.
4. Manage your energy and pace from the very beginning. Don't allow your enthusiasm to take control over you.
5. Turn your nervous energy into passion. Learn to channel it.
6. Focus on your listeners, not yourself.
7. Choose your favorite way of exercise and start doing it regularly.

Reflection Questions

1. Think of a time when your enthusiasm helped your message land, and a time when it may have overshadowed your point. What was different between the two moments?
2. How do you usually manage nerves or extra energy before a presentation? Which of the techniques in this chapter could you try next time?

3. What activities (like running, dancing, or exercise) could help you manage and balance your Fire energy outside of speaking?

4. How might shifting your focus from yourself to your audience change the way you experience nervousness?

Practical Tips

- **Channel Energy into Words:** Before your talk, write down the *one core message* you want your audience to take away. Having a clear focus keeps your fire pointed in the right direction.

- **Practice With a Timer:** Record yourself delivering a short speech at full Fire energy, then listen back to check pacing. If you're rushing, train by deliberately slowing sections down.

- **Anchor Yourself Physically:** Plant your feet firmly on the ground before you start. This physical grounding can balance emotional intensity with stability.

- **Build Recovery Pauses:** Mark in your notes where you'll pause after a key idea or story so your audience has time to absorb your passion.

- **Ask for Audience Feedback:** Invite a trusted colleague to tell you when your energy feels inspiring versus overwhelming. Outside perspective can reveal blind spots.

Fire in Action: Well-Known Examples

Russell Brunson

Brunson built his reputation selling from stage and teaching entrepreneurship. At first, his Fire energy often came across as too fast and overwhelming. Over time, he learned to pace his enthusiasm by building his presentations around stories and clear frameworks. By structuring his energy into predictable sequences — problem, story, solution, offer — he ensured that his speed and excitement worked *with* his message instead of running ahead of it. His development shows Fire speakers how intentional structure can tame raw intensity into persuasive clarity.

Grant Cardone

Cardone is known for his full-throttle Fire — loud, fast, and relentlessly energetic. Early in his career, this sometimes alienated audiences. But Cardone refined his Fire by anchoring it in repetition and structure. He developed signature phrases ("10X," "massive action") and built them into his talks so the audience had something solid to hold onto, even while his energy raced forward. His approach illustrates that Fire speakers can maximize impact when they pair intensity with consistent, repeatable messaging.

Tony Robbins

Robbins is one of the world's most recognized Fire speakers, famous for his explosive passion, physicality, and booming voice. But Robbins didn't just rely on raw energy. He studied breathing, pacing, and body control to keep his fire sustainable through hours-long events. He deliberately alternates between intensity and calm, guiding audiences through peaks and rests. His use of music, silence, and group exercises shows how Fire, when balanced with rhythm, becomes not just powerful but transformational.

CHAPTER 9
Develop Water

"May what I do flow from me like a river, no forcing and no holding back, the way it is with children."

— Rainer Maria Rilke

As soon as you define that your speaking energy is WATER and accept it, it's time to work on getting great at it.

Your voice is melodic, and your energy is flowing. These are your strengths, develop and use them. As Marcus Buckingham states in his books, First Break All The Rules and Put Your Strengths To Work, among others, when we focus on our strengths rather than our weaknesses, we develop them faster and more efficiently.

Work on your vocal variety and rhythm, as well as your voice in general. You have a predisposition for that, leverage it. Let's look at a few ways to develop this skill.

1. **Read out loud**

    It can be a book you're reading to your kids, any poem, or prose. Practice adjusting your pace, pitch, and volume to suit the meaning of the text.

Play with your voice as if it's a musical instrument. Emphasize certain words and enunciate the phrases. Change the rhythm when it feels appropriate.

2. **Practice tongue twisters**

Have you ever done that? This was one of my favorite activities with students when I was teaching English. However, tongue twisters are used not only by language learners but also by actors, news anchors, and speakers.

Tongue twisters help us with articulation, enunciation, and rhythm. They forge our clear speech free of mumbling.

Simply Google them, and you'll find a multitude of options.

3. **Develop your lung capacity**

To project your voice effectively, it's essential to practice various breathing exercises.

1. Practice speaking when running. You can rehearse your speech or just chat with a friend.
2. Try reading as many words as possible in one breath. Then keep increasing the length of the text you can read.
3. Recite the alphabet, inhaling before each letter and exhaling while pronouncing a letter.
4. Do the same with numbers.

5. Practice singing through a straw and make sure you feel the air coming out of the straw.
6. Hum "Happy birthday" and see if you can feel the vibration on your closed lips. If you don't, it means you're not projecting your voice correctly.

Now, let's examine a few problems that need to be addressed. You don't have to focus on them for too long, but it's important not to ignore them.

Speakers with WATER energy often speak as if they sing. Their speech flows like a river and they forget about pauses. It's crucial to develop self-awareness and always be present during your speech. Be present for the audience. Don't allow yourself to drift away into the smoothness of your flowing thoughts and words.

Stay aware of your listeners' reaction. Read the room and modify your speech as you go. It's easy for WATER speakers to be taken over by the stream just like FIRE speakers risk forgetting everything around them when they get excited.

Imagine jumping into a waterfall or a fast river. If you don't find a way to resist the flow, grab onto something and stop, it will carry you far into the areas you never planned to go. The same happens when you keep flowing without any stops.

Here's a tip I got from one of my podcast guests. He talked about the power of pauses. He says practice pauses when you're by yourself. Read or speak to yourself and make pauses much longer and more often than it's natural for you. It doesn't mean you'll be doing it when speaking in public. But you'll start getting used to them.

I can tell you from experience, it's a mindset shift. After practicing pauses when speaking by yourself, they become more comfortable. You start feeling them and sensing when it's time to speak.

Frankly speaking, I don't like pregnant pauses deliberately prolonged for effect. They feel unnatural to me. Nobody speaks like that in real life. Why pretend it's normal when presenting then? But it's definitely powerful to make good strong pauses that are natural to you and relevant to your content.

If the WATER speaking energy is well developed, such people will be the most balanced speakers. They are fast but not as intense as FIRE, flowing and gentle but steadier and more grounded than AIR; persuasive and strong but not as detached as EARTH may be.

Now, let's summarize. How can WATER energy speakers develop their skill and maximize their strengths?

1) Work on your vocal variety.
2) Use tongue twisters to work on your rhythm, play with pace, pitch, and volume.
3) Read out loud and do breathing exercises to develop your lung capacity.
4) Practice pauses, get comfortable with them.
5) Slow down and learn to read the room.

Summary:

WATER speakers thrive on flow, rhythm, and emotional connection. Their strength lies in creating a voice that feels like music — varied, melodic, and engaging. But the very gift of flow can also become a weakness if it never pauses or loses awareness of the audience. Developing Water energy means refining vocal variety, expanding lung capacity, and learning to use pauses with confidence. When balanced, Water speakers embody adaptability and connection, offering both emotional resonance and persuasive clarity.

Reflection Questions

1. When you speak, do you notice yourself flowing smoothly without pausing — or do you naturally include moments of stillness?
2. Which part of vocal variety (pace, pitch, volume, or rhythm) comes easiest to you, and which feels hardest to practice?
3. How do you usually "read the room"? What signals from your audience help you adjust your delivery?
4. If your speech style is musical, what might you do to add contrast — moments of quiet, stillness, or grounding?

Practical Tips

- **Record and Listen Back:** Record yourself reading a short text aloud. Play it back and note where your rhythm feels too even. Add intentional pauses or shifts to break the pattern.

- **Sing or Chant for Control:** Practice singing a simple tune or chanting a poem. It strengthens projection and teaches you to sustain breath while staying expressive.

- **Mark Pauses in Notes:** As you prepare a talk, insert dashes or slashes in your notes where you want to pause. Visual cues help train natural pacing.

- **Practice "Audience Check-Ins":** During conversations or presentations, consciously pause to look at faces. Notice if they seem engaged or drifting — then adjust tone or pacing.

- **Contrast Practice:** Read the same sentence three different ways — soft and slow, fast and loud, calm and steady. This builds flexibility and keeps you from defaulting into one rhythm.

Water in Action: Well-Known Examples

Lisa Nichols

Lisa is a powerful example of developed Water energy. Early in her speaking career, she often overflowed with raw emotion, but over time she learned to shape that emotion into storytelling with clear arcs. She trained her voice for range - shifting volume, speed, and tone to guide her audiences through both tears and laughter. Her growth illustrates how Water energy can be disciplined without losing authenticity, becoming even more compelling.

Maya Angelou

Maya Angelou refined her Water style through poetry and performance. Her melodic voice and emotional cadence were natural gifts, but she trained them further by reading aloud, reciting, and experimenting with rhythm. She demonstrated how a speaker can weave vulnerability and strength together to captivate audiences.

Simon Sinek

Sinek began as a thoughtful storyteller, but he worked on grounding his Water energy with clarity and structure. By blending his flowing, emotional delivery with clear frameworks ("Start with Why"), he ensured his ideas resonated beyond inspiration. He shows that Water energy, when developed, can both move hearts and sharpen minds.

CHAPTER 10
Develop Air

"I can't change the direction of the wind, but I can adjust my sails to always reach my destination." — Jimmy Dean

Have you ever heard someone speak with a calm, soothing voice? When you listen to it, you feel like everything is right with the world. They know their voice is powerful, even though it's not loud and not fast. Their power is in silence - in pauses, in whispers. It's because they've embraced their speaking energy and have worked on developing it.

Many people with AIR speaking energy are unaware of their power. They still think their introversion and calm nature make them unfit to be a speaker. But what they don't realize is that their innate ability to convey a message calmly is a huge advantage.

Therefore, the first step in developing your energy, my dear AIR speakers, is to embrace your style, believe in yourself, and start tapping into your power.

Now, how can you tap into it and utilize it to its full capacity?

Here are a few steps for you:

1. Find your natural and most comfortable pitch/volume/tempo of voice.

2. Practice projecting your voice so that even when you whisper, it's audible and clear.
3. Use your soothing voice in casual situations and observe the effect it has on people.
4. Embrace the beauty and power of your light, calming, soothing voice, and start leveraging it.
5. Listen to speakers on TED and find the ones with similar personalities to yours and a similar style of speaking. Write down their strengths, the ways they use their energy, and note to yourself what you can learn from them.

Let me tell you about one of my best friends who has AIR speaking energy. He can't stand public speaking and prefers his wife to do it instead of him when they have to present to big groups as a couple.

But at the same time, whenever he speaks, it's always witty, on point, and in a calm way. His speaking energy is his power. He is not trying to be like someone else. He doesn't talk much, and yet every word out of his mouth counts.

That's the essence of every speaker with this beautiful energy. If you've embraced it, tapped into it, and started developing it.

Many people with AIR speaking energy are deep, intuitive personalities, great thinkers, and experts at reading people.

Maybe you weren't aware of such an ability. Start observing and paying closer attention to your strengths.

Your introversion is your power. There are multiple ways for you to use it in speaking and presenting.

Define the strongest sides of your personality. Take time to understand your most powerful qualities. Is it empathy? Discernment? Intellect? Analytical thinking? What comes easily to you and feels incredibly natural?

Knowing your personality and strengths will help you develop your unique style of speaking and utilize your AIR energy effectively.

I know it's important for all of us to be aware of our strengths and develop them. So, why am I discussing it in this chapter? Because it's especially important for our AIR speakers.

I know too many introverted people with quiet personalities who have given up on themselves in terms of speaking. They decided it wasn't meant for them because it's not in their nature to talk charismatically in public.

And even though they have a lot to say, they bury that beautiful message deep in their heart and deprive the world of hearing it.

It only seems that our AIR speakers aren't born for the stage because of their calm nature. It's a stereotype and an archaism that all speakers need to be loud and emotional. In reality, some of the best ones are actually quiet and introverted.

Their peaceful, soothing demeanor is their superpower. And the incredible ability to manage their emotions is what sets them apart.

So, if your speaking energy is AIR, develop your ability to convey the message calmly. That's what you'll be known for.

Let's summarize. What have we talked about in this chapter?

What are the ways AIR speakers can develop their speaking energy?

1. Embrace the power of your calm way of speaking. See it as a strength, not a weakness.
2. Find your natural and most comfortable pitch/volume/tempo of voice.
3. Practice projecting your voice so that even when you whisper, it's audible and clear.
4. Define your personality strengths. Write them down and strategize on how to develop them.
5. When you know your strengths, determine your most natural style of speaking.
6. Celebrate your introversion and calm personality. Use it as a superpower.
7. Make sure you don't bury your message and desire to speak up. Share it with the world.
8. Help others to manage their emotions, resolve conflicts, and deal with anxiety.

Summary: Developing Air

AIR speakers carry quiet strength - their calm, soothing presence and intuitive insight draw listeners in. The challenge is not to "be louder," but to recognize introversion and subtlety as superpowers. Developing Air energy means embracing your natural style, learning to project with clarity, and leaning into personal strengths like empathy, discernment, or analytical thinking. When cultivated, Air energy transforms stereotypes of "quiet = weak" into the reality of "quiet = magnetic."

Reflection Questions

1. Do you sometimes view your calm nature as a weakness rather than a strength?
2. When have people leaned in or paid closer attention because of your quiet delivery?
3. What strengths - empathy, discernment, intellect - feel most natural to you, and how could you use them in your speaking?
4. What fears keep you from sharing your voice more often?

Practical Tips

- **Whisper Practice:** Try delivering part of your talk at a whisper while still projecting clearly. It teaches you to maintain clarity and presence without raising volume.
- **Small-Group Testing:** Share your message first in small, safe groups. This builds confidence gradually while reinforcing that your style connects.

- **Silent Presence Drill:** Before speaking, practice standing silently in front of the room for 10-15 seconds, making eye contact. This strengthens comfort with stillness and presence.
- **Strength-Based Journaling:** Each week, write down one personal strength you used in communication (empathy, analysis, intuition). Track how it shapes your style.
- **Seek Role Models:** Revisit TED Talks or interviews of speakers with gentle styles. Note exactly how they project calm while staying impactful.

Air in Action: Well-Known Examples

Susan Cain

Cain began as a quiet, introverted professional who avoided the spotlight. But to share her message on introversion, she studied speaking, practiced relentlessly, and leaned into her natural calm. Her TED Talk became one of the most-viewed in history because she didn't force herself into Fire energy - she trusted her quiet style. Cain's development shows Air speakers that practice plus authenticity leads to powerful influence.

Fred Rogers

Rogers cultivated his signature calm presence through intentional practice. He slowed his voice, embraced long pauses, and used gentle eye contact to make children feel safe. He didn't bury his quietness, he magnified it into his brand of influence. His development shows that stillness and simplicity, when chosen deliberately, can be a speaker's greatest strength.

Steven Spielberg

Spielberg is primarily known as a filmmaker, but his Air energy is evident in how he communicates. Unlike many directors who dominate with authority, Spielberg often speaks softly, with humility and thoughtfulness. Early in his career, he had to learn to project confidence despite his quiet demeanor earning respect by listening deeply, asking precise questions, and letting his vision speak through storytelling. His development shows Air speakers that influence doesn't always come from commanding the room; sometimes it's about creating space where others feel seen and inspired.

CHAPTER 11
Develop Earth

"He who wants to persuade should put his trust not in the right argument, but in the right word. The power of sound has always been greater than the power of sense." — Joseph Conrad

More than 22 years ago, I met Maia for the first time. Two years later, we started working in the same team, and our friendship began. She soon became one of my best friends and basically my family.

I was in my early 20s, and she was 8 years older. I was emotional, enthusiastic, and had lots of energy. She could always control her emotions and speak with calm confidence.

Whenever I saw her teach and heard her speak, I felt the difference in our styles and thought I needed to emulate her. Her style of speaking seemed more professional. And mine, on the other hand, felt infantile, not serious enough, and all over the place.

That's when I started quenching my energy. I denied my unique style and tried adopting my friend's, because my natural way of speaking didn't seem good enough for me.

Looking back, I know it was a mistake. It took me about a decade to realize it wasn't me. Trying to be like someone else almost made me kill my strengths and silence my gifts. However, my enthusiastic, emotional, and a bit crazy nature kept shining through any door behind which I would try closing it.

Finally, I was able to find myself. It took a lot of inner work, multiple personality tests, help from coaches, mentors, and friends.

That's why I'm so passionate about inspiring you to define, develop, and demonstrate your speaking energy.

Everything I just shared can be summed up in one phrase: Earth speaking energy is extremely strong and desirable to many.

My friend Maia is one of the best representatives of this style.

So, how can you develop your EARTH speaking style? Let's dive into it.

First, ensure you understand your current position in the development process. Do you feel the power of your speaking energy? Have you embraced and harnessed it? Do you always speak with confidence and persuasion? Have you honed your skill to pause at the right moment and for the right amount of time (neither too long nor too short)?

If any of the questions above got a negative answer, it's time to work on your voice, style, and speaking energy.

Your biggest strengths as an EARTH speaker are confidence and persuasion, executive presence, and the strength of an argument.

If you don't feel competent enough in these areas, it's possible you have not developed them yet. Just remember, you have it in you. Start working on these skills, and their improvement will skyrocket.

A few reminders on how to develop your persuasiveness.

1. **Use a low-pitched voice**

   Subconsciously, we perceive the low pitch of anybody's voice as more convincing. It seems the person knows what they are talking about.

   You don't have to lower it too much. Make sure it feels comfortable and natural for you. Use the variety of pitch when playing with your voice.

   Your higher-pitched voice is useful in situations where you desire to establish a connection with the audience. Keep it in mind and practice self-awareness using the right pitch in appropriate situations.

2. **Use falling inflection**

   As you know, we use the rising inflection of our voice when we ask questions. That's why if you use it when making a statement, it sounds as if you're not sure and asking for approval.

   Make your voice fall at the end of the statement. It will make you sound more persuasive.

3. Make sure you believe in what you're saying

That's when your passions show up. People can sense if there's any doubt or disbelief.

You might not be aware of it yourself. But if you're not convinced, your body language will show it.

Almost invisible micro expressions will give you away. So make sure you first persuade yourself and then share it with others.

4. Avoid saying phrases "I think", "It seems to me", "In my opinion", "Perhaps", etc

These are great phrases to use when your goal is to make a connection and build a rapport.

However, when you're making a statement with the purpose of persuading, they will weaken your argument.

5. Simplify your content.

Use simple sentence structures and understandable words. Don't try to sound smart. Your intelligence will be evident in the ideas and solutions you propose.

Avoid using passive voice whenever possible and refrain from using specific terminology.

These are the persuasion tips. There's much more to the EARTH speaking energy. Another strength of speakers with this style is executive presence.

If you know it's your energy but you don't feel like you've developed a great presence, it's time to work on it.

I definitely recommend to read Amy Cuddy's "Presence" and Sylvia Ann Hewlett's "Executive Presence".

Explore this strength of yours and start paying attention to how you carry yourself when you're with other people. Be aware of your presence, of your effect on them. Observe people's reaction to you.

Having an executive presence doesn't mean you have to be haughty and cold. It's a perfect combination of confidence, self-awareness, emotional intelligence, and being present in the moment.

Let's look at all the techniques again:

1. Use a low-pitched voice.
2. Use falling inflection.
3. Believe in what you're saying.
4. Stop using phrases that dilute the strength of your argument.
5. Simplify your content.
6. Develop presence by increasing your self-awareness.
7. Be observant.

Summary:

EARTH speakers are steady, persuasive, and confident. Their power lies in the weight of their words, the authority of their presence, and the trust they inspire. But this energy doesn't develop on its own. It requires awareness - choosing the right pitch, mastering inflection, and eliminating weak language. When paired with executive presence and emotional intelligence, Earth energy becomes deeply persuasive without arrogance. Developing this style is about cultivating grounded authority while remaining approachable and human.

Reflection Questions

1. Do you believe in the message you're sharing or do you sometimes hear uncertainty in your own words?
2. How conscious are you of your voice (pitch, inflection, phrasing) when you speak?
3. When people listen to you, do they experience you as calm and confident, or distant and rigid?
4. What small adjustments could you make to strengthen both your persuasiveness and your presence?

Practical Tips

- **Record for Inflection Awareness:** Record yourself reading a short statement. Notice if your voice rises at the end (sounding unsure). Practice lowering your inflection on strong points.
- **Develop Presence Beyond Speaking:** Pay attention to posture, eye contact, and stillness. Earth energy is as much about how you *stand* as what you say.

- **Practice "Convince Yourself First":** Before delivering a talk, spend five minutes affirming why your message matters to you personally. Your conviction will show.
- **Simplify to Amplify:** Challenge yourself to explain a complex idea in one or two short sentences. This builds clarity and authority.
- **Ask for Feedback on Presence:** Invite a colleague or friend to share how your presence makes them feel - reassured, intimidated, inspired? Their perspective can guide your refinement.

Earth in Action: Well-Known Examples

Angela Merkel

Merkel developed her Earth energy through restraint and pragmatism. Early on, she was criticized for being too understated, but over time she turned her quiet authority into a strength. She cultivated trust by staying calm in crises, choosing precise words, and allowing her steadiness to speak louder than volume. Merkel shows that Earth presence can grow stronger by leaning into consistency and composure.

Brené Brown

Brené's Earth style didn't come from projecting power in the traditional sense, but from combining grounded research with personal vulnerability. She worked on simplifying complex ideas and delivering them with warmth and clarity. Her TED Talk and books demonstrate how Earth speakers can be both authoritative and relatable by connecting research with real human stories.

Nelson Mandela

Nelson Mandela developed his Earth energy through patience and resilience. His speeches carried weight because they were rooted in conviction and simplicity. Instead of fiery delivery, he spoke slowly, deliberately, and with moral authority. Years of discipline and reflection shaped his style, showing how Earth energy matures when grounded in values and inner strength.

CHAPTER 12
All Four Types In Review

"Be yourself; everyone else is already taken" — Oscar Wilde.

Now, let's take a bird view and look at all the types at once. What are the differences and similarities in the development of all speaking energies?

As you remember, they are all connected. And the way you develop your type of speaking can be similar to the speaking energy that's next to yours.

Before we go any further, I'd like for you to understand one important concept. There are specific tips for your type. It's important to realize what your strengths are and focus on developing them because your growth in those areas will be phenomenal. I also listed some weaknesses specific to certain types. You can work on those as well to get the best of your personality and create your speaking style.

However, if you'd like to become a well-rounded speaker, check out all the tips for other speaking energies as well. And see, what techniques you'd like to use to grow as a presenter.

Don't become someone else. Be yourself. However, choose what features of other types you'd like to adopt, embrace and develop. It'll help you speak with even more power.

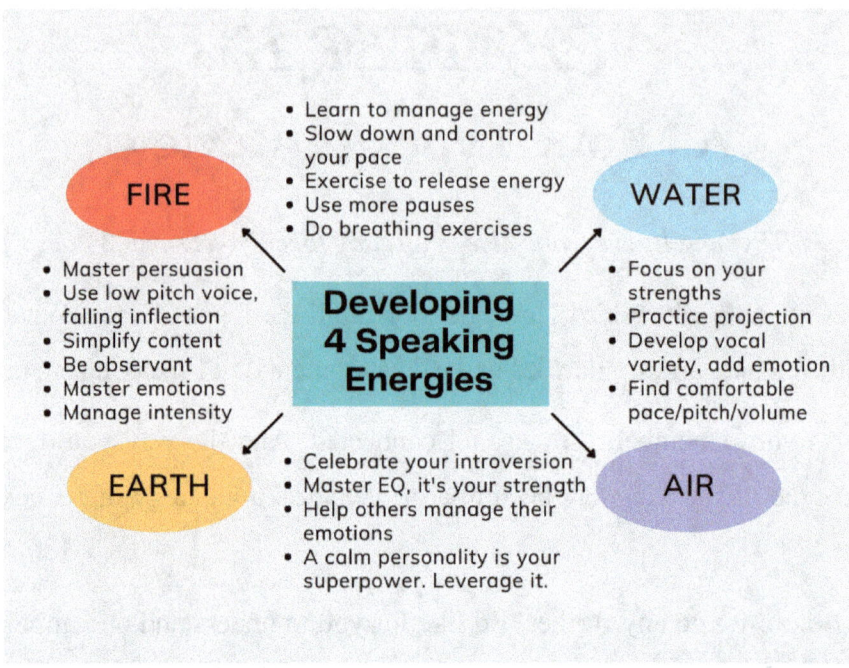

Now, let's look at the chart of all energies and how you can develop them.

As you can see, each speaking energy shares special tips and techniques with two other energies.

Of course, it doesn't hurt to apply everything, no matter what your type is. But it's wiser to start developing your speaking energy and only then see if there's anything in other types you'd like to adopt and work on.

Let me reiterate to emphasize the point.

- Your style of speaking is unique and is based on your personality type.

- Your speaking energy depends on who you are as a person.
- Don't ever try to be someone else.
- Find what feels natural to you, your most authentic way of expressing yourself, and master it.
- You don't have to be an extrovert or a highly energetic person to be a great speaker. Your style might be as powerful. Just find that power and tap into it.
- **When you've mastered YOUR speaking energy**, start working on becoming a well-rounded speaker. Adopt your favorite techniques from other styles to utilize them in appropriate situations.

This concludes Part II: Develop. In the next section, you will learn how to demonstrate your speaking energy and always present with P.O.W.E.R.

Reflection Questions

1. Which of the four energies do you most identify with right now, and how has your view of it changed since the start of this book?
2. Looking across all four types, which strengths from *other* energies would you most like to borrow or adopt?
3. What personal habits or patterns hold you back from fully stepping into your speaking energy?
4. How do you want your audience to feel after hearing you speak, and which energy helps you create that effect most naturally?

Practical Tips

- **Create a Development Map:** Write down your core energy, your top three strengths, and one weakness you'd like to work on. This becomes your roadmap for practice.

- **Blend, Don't Replace:** Pick one technique from another energy (e.g., Fire's pauses, Water's vocal flow, Air's stillness, Earth's authority) and experiment with adding it to your next presentation.

- **Review and Refine:** After each talk, reflect on whether you stayed authentic to your core energy while experimenting with new techniques.

- **Anchor in Authenticity:** Whenever you feel tempted to copy another speaker, remind yourself: "My power comes from being fully myself."

- **Practice Across Contexts:** Try using your speaking energy not only in speeches but also in everyday life - meetings, conversations, teaching moments. Development grows fastest when it's consistent.

PART III
DEMONSTRATE

CHAPTER 13
You Are Charismatic

"Charisma is a sparkle in people that money can't buy. It's an invisible energy with visible effects." — *Marianne Williamson*

Once, when I was in second grade, my class was preparing a performance for the whole school. I remember how I collected all my courage and marched towards two teachers standing near the window, discussing something.

"I can sing a song", I said with hope. My heart was pounding, but my eyes were shining with anticipation.

They skeptically looked at me with slight irritation that I had interrupted their conversation.

"Ok, show us", one of them said.

I sang a Ukrainian National song that I had known since I was a baby. It was far from perfect, of course, but not bad either.

They looked at each other with a smirk and said, "Oh, it's ok, we don't need another song."

And this kind of attitude from teachers followed me all the way through middle school. I was invisible to them. Unnoticeable.

In fifth grade, my class participated in a school competition. All of us were in a big auditorium. A few representatives from each class were on the stage. Suddenly, one of our classmates had to drop out.

I went to the teacher right away and eagerly said, "I can go take her place."

She squeezed her eyes, looked me up and down, and said: "Mm, no. You go." And she pointed to another girl.

I was devastated. Am I not good enough? What's wrong with me?

Don't we all ask ourselves these kinds of questions at least once in our lives?

Things started changing for me when my family moved from the cold northern city of Murmansk to the beautiful country of Ukraine.

It was a new environment, new people around me, and a clean slate to start building one's reputation and character.

I was 14 years old when I wrote in my journal:

"I want to be a journalist and an interpreter. That's why I need to build confidence."

And I started doing it. Step by step. Day after day. As a voracious reader, I devoured books and magazine articles that eventually changed my life.

One of them discussed the postures and sleep positions of confident individuals. "But what if I go the other way? - I thought - What if I sleep in this position and train myself to stand a certain way? Maybe it'll help me build confidence."

And it did. I completely changed the way I slept; I adopted the postures of confident people. I taught myself to stand, think, and act like a confident person. And after years of developing this skill, confidence became one of my strengths.

Little did I know these ideas and techniques would become the cornerstone of the future research by Amy Cuddy and Harvard University. But I would find out about that much later. And while I still had ways to go in terms of internalizing self-worth and building self-esteem, it was a good start.

Back then, my greatest joy, pride, and accomplishment was delivering my valedictorian speech at graduation. An invisible girl became one of the top performers in her class and was invited to speak to all graduates, parents, and teachers.

That speech became the pinnacle of my confidence work and ignited a new passion for public speaking. A shy, unnoticeable, ugly duckling was able to inspire a crowd.

Standing on the stage, seeing the smiles on people's faces and the sparks in their eyes, showed me the power and beauty of public speaking.

Now I have worked with hundreds of clients from 23 countries and counting.

In 2020, I was named one of the Top 500 entrepreneurs by Brainz magazine, alongside Simon Sinek and Jim Kwik.

In 2021 and 2022, Tony Robbins and Dean Graziosi featured me at their annual World Summit.

Not too bad for an invisible girl from Ukraine.

———

This is my story of developing charisma, transforming from a shy person to a confident and outspoken one.

What about you? Can you call yourself a charismatic speaker and leader?

Even if your answer is 'no' and you still doubt you have charisma, you can develop it.

Olivia Fox Cabane, in her book The Charisma Myth, argues that charisma is a learnable behavior and a skill anybody can develop.

She distinguishes three main components of charisma: power, presence, and warmth.

And that's what we will dive deeper into in the next chapter, but from the perspective of a speaker.

Summary:

Charisma isn't about being born special — it's about developing confidence, presence, and authenticity over time. What feels invisible or unnoticed in childhood can become magnetic when we choose to step into our strengths, build confidence through practice, and share our voices with the world. Just as confidence can be trained, so can charisma. Every speaker has the potential to shine when they learn to combine presence, power, and warmth in their unique way.

Reflection Questions

1. Have you ever felt "invisible" in a group or overlooked when you wanted to contribute? How did that experience shape you?
2. What steps have you already taken to build confidence, and which ones have been most effective?
3. When you speak, do people experience you as more powerful, more warm, or more present? Which of these feels natural to you, and which could you strengthen?
4. If charisma is learnable, what's one small habit you could begin today to grow your presence?

Practical Tips

- **Confidence Posture Exercise:** Stand tall, with open shoulders and lifted head, for two minutes before your next presentation. This triggers physiological changes that support confidence.
- **Daily "Visibility" Practice:** Do one small thing each day that makes you seen: ask a question in a meeting, share a story with a friend, or volunteer for a role.

- **Feedback on Presence:** Ask a trusted colleague, "When I speak, do I come across as confident, approachable, or both?" Their perception can help you refine.
- **Warmth Practice:** In conversations, consciously smile and soften your tone once. Small adjustments in warmth build connection quickly.
- **Charisma Journal:** At the end of each day, jot down one moment when you felt charismatic (even if tiny) and what created it. Over time, you'll build a map of what works for you.

CHAPTER 14
Speak With P.O.W.E.R.

"Speech is power: speech is to persuade, to convert, to compel."
-Ralph Waldo Emerson

Let's assume that by now you know your Speaking Energy. What is it? FIRE, WATER, AIR, or EARTH?

And let's say you started developing it. Mind you, this stage never ends because there's always room for growth.

As soon as you develop your speaking energy to a certain degree, you are ready to demonstrate it.

Can you feel it? Can you feel the freedom of sharing your voice? Not trying to speak like someone else, but perfecting and showcasing your own unique, beautiful style, with amazing speaking energy.

That's the power. That's charisma.

And in this chapter, we'll look into five components of P.O.W.E.R. - Presence, Ownership, Winner's mindset, Energy, and Resilience.

Let's start with PRESENCE.

What springs to your mind right away when you hear the word? For some people, it will be mindfulness and meditation, being grounded. For others, it's active listening. Perhaps for you, it's holding a child or watching the waves crash on the shore.

Presence is being in the moment right there, wherever you are. Whatever you're experiencing. Be there. Are you with people? Give them your full attention. Are you by yourself? Focus on your sensations. Look around. Take it all in.

Presence is powerful because it gives us an enormous amount of information. We miss so much in life by hurrying, by looking either to the past or to the future. However, if you ground yourself in the present moment, the calmness you'll exude as a result will be that charisma everyone's talking about.

Now let's talk about OWNERSHIP.

What does it mean to own your message? It's when you and your speech become one. You own it and it owns you. That's how much you care about it.

You can feel every moment of your speech with the deepest, smallest fibers of your heart. There's no need to memorize your speech and perform it. It's a part of you now. All you've got to do is open your mouth and let it flow like a river.

And you know what will be the result? Your passion, your enthusiasm will shine through. It's the best way to show how much you care about the message and purpose of your presentation.

Own it, and there won't be any room for failure. No, let me scratch that. You'll make mistakes and fail sometimes, but it won't matter because it's just a part of life. Because you're a normal human being, and your passion will be much more important than your perfection.

What's next? WINNER'S MINDSET

Frankly speaking, Mindset should be at the forefront. Everything starts with mindset - presence, power, confidence, and even our speaking energy.

Maria was a client of mine several years ago. When she shared her problem, it was obvious we needed to work on her mindset first. Maria is a brilliant woman who came to the US in her 20s, worked hard on getting a degree, built her business from the ground up, and still felt insecure about her accent.

"They look down at me when I start talking," she shared about her colleagues. "I can't speak with enough confidence. I think people misunderstand me because of my accent."

"Everyone has an accent!' I told her. "You have an amazing story of going from nothing to incredible success. People need to hear it!"

And that's when we started working on her mindset. She learned, practiced, and looked at herself differently, developing confidence as a speaker.

Now, Maria inspires hundreds of people in her circle of influence to pursue their dreams and achieve seemingly unattainable goals. Give her a little time, and she'll be inspiring thousands.

So, how do we build a Winner's Mindset?

First of all, you've got to realize what's holding you back in speaking. Are there any doubts, fears, or imposter syndrome?

Write down every obstacle that is holding you back. Once you have a list, review it and try to identify the underlying reasons for these doubts. Typically, the root lies in a limiting belief formed from a negative experience.

Achieving self-awareness in this area is the first and most powerful step. Bring those dark forces into the light so you can overcome them.

Now, this is my favorite: ENERGY.

You've already defined your speaking energy and hopefully started developing it. It's time to demonstrate it.

Imagine that you're walking alone in the field. You can see miles away and know for sure there's not a single person anywhere close to you. Suddenly, you're coming to a meadow with beautiful flowers everywhere and a big stump right in the middle of it.

You get closer to the stump, climb on top of it, and look around. Not a soul. Nobody to judge you. You can't fail.

You feel incredible freedom and lightness. Your mouth opens, and words start flowing like a river.

Why did I describe this scenario to you? I want you to feel your most natural, authentic self. Who are you when no one's watching? That's your unique energy.

When you demonstrate it in your speech, it feels right, light, and free. You show up as your best self, and everyone listening can sense it. Your charisma becomes obvious because you're not faking it. You embody it.

And finally, RESILIENCE

What does it mean to be a resilient speaker?

Numerous situations in the world of speaking could potentially go wrong. If you don't develop resilience, they will break you.

What do you do if something unexpected happens? Let's say your laptop doesn't work or the cords don't fit, and you can't use your presentation. How would you react to that?

What if there's a difficult person in the audience and you keep getting objections and hard questions? Can you handle it?

That's resilience. You can bounce back no matter what happens. It's flexibility and elasticity - the skill to speak impromptu, be spontaneous, and resourceful.

Now you know what P.O.W.E.R. stands for in speaking. Which of these components do you need to work on so that you can demonstrate your speaking energy with power?

Summary:

P.O.W.E.R. is the way we bring our speaking energy to life. Presence roots us in the moment, Ownership makes the message truly ours, a Winner's Mindset fuels confidence, Energy reveals our authentic style, and Resilience ensures we keep going no matter what happens. When these five elements come together, our charisma becomes visible and our voice gains lasting impact. Speaking with P.O.W.E.R. is not about perfection — it's about showing up fully, authentically, and with courage.

Reflection Questions

1. Which of the five components of P.O.W.E.R. feels most natural to you? Which feels most challenging?
2. Think back to a time when you "owned" your message. How did it change the way people received it?
3. What limiting beliefs or doubts hold you back from demonstrating your energy with confidence?
4. How do you usually react when something goes wrong during a presentation? What would resilience look like in that moment?
5. If your audience could describe your presence in one word, what would you want it to be?

Practical Tips

- **Presence Drill:** Before a talk, take two minutes to observe your environment - sights, sounds, and sensations - to anchor yourself in the present moment.

- **Ownership Rehearsal:** Instead of memorizing your speech word-for-word, practice telling it as if it's a personal story. This helps it flow naturally.

- **Mindset Reset:** Write down your biggest speaking fears. Then reframe each into a positive belief ("They'll judge me" → "They're here to hear my message").

- **Energy Test:** Practice your speech alone in a room, then again with one trusted friend. Notice if your delivery feels authentic in both cases - adjust until it does.

- **Resilience Practice:** Intentionally rehearse without slides or notes once. Train yourself to keep speaking even if technology fails.

CHAPTER 15
Demonstrate Fire

"Enthusiasm is that ingredient of vitality mixed with a firm belief in what you are doing that ensures the success of any project you undertake."
— *Dale Carnegie*

Let's focus on each speaking energy and discuss how you can demonstrate it to the world. We'll start with FIRE.

When was the last time you were sitting around the campfire with your friends? Perhaps someone was playing the guitar, while others sang a song. The fire was giving you warmth and coziness. It was powerful and beautiful.

But imagine if it got out of control. How much damage could it do to the forest and everyone around?

The same way you need to keep your FIRE under *control* if it's your speaking energy.

Show your enthusiasm and passion, but stay in control of your emotions. Always be aware of the feelings boiling inside, express them with moderation, and don't let them explode and overwhelm your listeners.

A few years ago, I was looking for a new job. As some of you know, it's a painstakingly long and tedious process that often leads to disappointment. After several months of sending out resumes and attending interviews, I was finally at an assessment conference alongside nine other applicants. It was the final stage of the process, and my chances looked pretty good. One of the tasks at the conference was to prepare and present a brief workshop. "That's easy", I thought. I've done it hundreds of times. There's no need to say I was nervous. Who wouldn't be? And at the same time, I was extremely passionate about the topic of my workshop. Can you imagine what this fiery mixture produced? I couldn't contain my energy and enthusiasm. The voice was too loud; the pace was too fast. And that's exactly the feedback I got from the decision-makers after the presentation.

I didn't get the job. But I learned a powerful lesson. Control your emotions and don't let them take away your opportunities.

So, if the first word you needed to embrace were 'control', the next one would be 'adapt'. When meeting with people whose energy is quieter, *adapt* to them, especially if it's an important negotiation. Learn to be flexible; it may become one of your most valuable qualities.

Let's take my example of giving a workshop during an interview process in an attempt to get a new job. I wasn't able to control my emotions and adapt my energy to the needs of the audience. The stakes were high. It was crucial to research and understand the expectations of the decision-makers, and then adapt my delivery accordingly. However, I didn't do it and blew my chance.

How could I have done it? I could have slowed down, used more pauses in my speech, and shown more executive presence instead of childish enthusiasm.

And the third tip for demonstrating your FIRE is *release*. After you have trained your mind and body to control your fire and manage your emotions, after you have learned to adapt, in the right circumstances, you can release all your passion and enthusiasm. Show it in all its glory. Set it free!

Remember, I told you I wanted to be like my friend with EARTH speaking energy? I was extremely intentional about molding myself into someone I was not. And it led me to suppress some of my best qualities: passion, enthusiasm, playfulness, and warmth.

It took me years to realize how wrong I was. Finally, I saw that my FIRE was my superpower and putting it out would be a crime and a disaster.

If your speaking energy is FIRE, all you need to do is know how to show that fire in all its beauty and power. You've got to make sure it doesn't hurt anybody or burn any bridges and connections you've built.

Summary:

FIRE speakers shine when they show enthusiasm and passion, but only if they stay in *control*. Too much energy can overwhelm an audience, while intentional pacing and adaptation build trust and impact. Demonstrating Fire is about balance: controlling the flame, *adapting* to your audience, and then *releasing* passion at the right moment. When channeled well, Fire energy warms, inspires, and motivates without burning bridges.

Reflection Questions

1. Think of a time when your enthusiasm carried you away. How did it affect your audience?
2. How comfortable are you at adapting your delivery when the room's energy is quieter than yours?
3. What does "release" look like for you, in which situations can you let your passion shine fully?
4. Are there moments when you've hidden your Fire out of fear of being "too much"? What was lost in doing that?

Practical Tips

- **The Two-Speed Practice:** Rehearse your talk once at your natural fast pace, then again deliberately slower with pauses. Notice how your message changes.
- **Anchor Phrases:** Choose 2–3 sentences in your speech where you intentionally slow down, lower your voice, and make eye contact - this grounds your Fire.
- **Mirror the Room:** At the start of a meeting or presentation, match your audience's energy for the first minute, then gradually bring them up to your level.
- **Release With Purpose:** Save your full passion for key stories or calls to action so your fire feels intentional rather than constant.
- **Energy Outlet:** Before speaking, use physical movement (push-ups, a walk, stretching) to release excess energy and come in balanced.

Fire in Action: Well-Known Examples

Tony Robbins

Robbins is the ultimate example of controlled Fire. His passion is unmistakable — the booming voice, the physical movement, the intensity, but notice how he builds in moments of control. He lowers his voice, pauses, and lets silence land before ramping back up. That control makes the bursts of fire even more impactful.

Gary Vaynerchuk

Gary V is known for unfiltered enthusiasm and raw honesty, but what makes him effective is his ability to adapt. When speaking to business leaders, he tempers his speed and sharpness, slowing down to explain his ideas. That flexibility keeps his Fire from overwhelming and helps it resonate with different audiences.

Russell Brunson

Brunson demonstrates the release of Fire at exactly the right time. On stage, his storytelling and frameworks build steadily, but when it's time to make a call to action, he unleashes all his enthusiasm. That release of passion carries the audience with him - they feel the heat and want to move with him.

CHAPTER 16

Demonstrating Water

"Those who flow as life flows know they need no other force." — Lao Tzu

Your biggest superpower is your flexibility, fluidity, and ability to speak as if you're singing a song. Leverage this unique ability and show it to the world.

Just like FIRE, you need to remember three magic words for an effective demonstration of your power and speaking energy.

The first one is *embrace*. You have to allow the beauty of your energy to show itself. Embrace its power and demonstrate it.

Most people don't realize how much potential they have for speaking. Your type is the most balanced one. It gets its power from the freedom it possesses.

So set it free and embrace it fully. That's who you are - a powerful energy that adapts easily to the audience around.

Have you read "Now, Discover Your Strengths" by Marcus Buckingham and Donald Clifton? Their main idea is that if we focus on developing our areas of strength, the growth is exponentially faster and more intense than if we focus on neutralizing our weaknesses.

Your voice and energy are your strengths. You might be a shy person or someone who hasn't yet discovered this gift within you. It's time to embrace yourself fully and leverage this amazing talent.

The second magic word is *flow*. It's your superpower. Use the gentleness of your voice and let it flow in the right direction. Sometimes this flow will be like a fast stream in the woods or a fierce waterfall. At other times, it will be a slow and quiet current.

You will know how to adapt your energy because it's one of your strengths. Trust your intuition, listen to your gut, and go with the flow.

The third word for you, my powerful WATER speaker, is *enchant*. Thanks to the melody of your voice and the fluidity of your energy, the sound and rhythm of your speech have the potential to captivate listeners and hold their attention.

In order to tap into that ability, make sure there's no tension in your body. Relax all muscles, trust your voice, and let it out gently, like a song. There shouldn't be much intensity in your voice. Your enthusiasm is soft and flowing, unlike that of speakers with fire energy.

Summary:

WATER speakers demonstrate their power through balance, adaptability, and melody. When they *embrace* their natural style, they step into the confidence of who they are. When they allow themselves to *flow*, they adapt to the moment and guide the audience with ease. And when they learn to *enchant*, their voice becomes music - captivating, soothing, and unforgettable. Water energy is at its best when it is both free and intentional.

Reflection Questions

1. Do you find it easy or difficult to embrace your natural speaking style without trying to be someone else?

2. When you speak, does your energy feel more like a waterfall, a stream, or a calm river? How does that affect your audience?

3. Have you ever noticed your voice enchanting or soothing people? What did you do in that moment that made it work?

4. Where do you sense tension in your body when speaking, and how might releasing it allow more flow?

Practical Tips

- **Voice-as-Music Practice:** Record yourself reading a passage aloud. Then listen and notice the natural rhythm and melody. Practice emphasizing words to create a gentle rise and fall, like a song.

- **Flow Rehearsal:** Practice giving the same message three times - once fast and energetic, once slow and calm, and once somewhere in between. Notice how your flow changes the audience's perception.

- **Relaxation Check:** Before speaking, scan your body from head to toe. Drop your shoulders, unclench your jaw, and release tension so your voice can move freely.

- **Pauses as Currents:** Use pauses as the natural spaces between waves. They allow your message to breathe and keep listeners captivated without rushing.
- **Audience Connection:** Tune into your audience's energy and let it guide your flow adjusting speed, tone, and intensity to meet them where they are.

Water in Action: Well-Known Examples

Simon Sinek

Sinek demonstrates Water energy through his flowing, conversational style. He rarely rushes - instead, his words unfold like a steady current, inviting listeners to reflect with him. By embracing his thoughtful tone and using rhythm to guide ideas forward, he enchants audiences into seeing the "why" behind every message.

Maya Angelou

Her voice was a stream of strength and gentleness. Whether reading poetry or speaking in interviews, she embraced her calm power, flowed naturally, and enchanted audiences with warmth and truth.

Princess Diana

Known for her compassion and softness, Diana's Water energy was expressed in her gentle tone and empathetic presence. She didn't need to speak loudly, her sincerity enchanted hearts across the world.

CHAPTER 17
Demonstrating Air

"If a man has enough power, he can speak softly and everyone will listen."
— *Jake Roberts*

The biggest issue with AIR speakers is that they don't see their genius. They don't believe they have what it takes to be a great speaker. In truth, theirs is the most unique and underutilized power - the ability to deliver a message in a calm, soothing manner.

If AIR is your speaking energy, don't you dare hide it from people. The world needs you. Demonstrate it. Show it off. Share it with others. You'll be able to help so many people just by opening your mouth and letting peace envelop your listeners.

So, what are YOUR three magic words you want to ask? Here they are.

The first one is *believe*. Yes, believe in yourself, in your ability to speak with incredible and unique power. Believe that your voice transforms lives and your message has the potential to change the world. Believe that imposter syndrome is something we all experience because we are open to growth, to doing something new, and stepping out of our comfort zone.

I mentioned my client earlier, who thought he had to speak like Tony Robbins, despite his personality being completely different from that of Tony Robbins. He needed to believe in the strength of his unique voice, his speaking style, and his speaking energy. And as soon as he did, everything changed for him.

The next word is *soothe*. I said it before, and I'll say it again. It's your superpower to speak with a calming voice and help others conquer their emotions.

I want YOU to see it as a strength as well. Because many AIR speakers I know don't believe in their abilities. They are introverts and have a ridiculous idea that only extroverts are powerful speakers. That's so far from the truth.

You are someone people need nowadays when there's so much hype everywhere. Your calming, soothing energy brings peace and serenity to our minds, serving as a healing balm for our nerves.

The third magic word for people with AIR speaking energy is *pace*. As soon as you realize how powerful your energy is, you'll start getting more and more confident in it. And the best way for you to exude confidence is to pace yourself.

Speak more slowly, making pauses in the right places, and feel less nervous. Don't hurry. Breathe in, hold your breath, breathe out. And continue speaking as if all the time in the world belongs to you.

Summary:

AIR speakers demonstrate their power through quiet confidence and calming presence. When they *believe* in their unique voice, they step beyond imposter syndrome and embrace their natural gift. When they *soothe*, they bring peace and clarity in a world full of noise. And when they *pace* themselves, their stillness becomes magnetic, allowing every word to land with weight and intention. AIR energy reminds us that soft does not mean weak, it means unforgettable.

Reflection Questions

1. Do you sometimes dismiss your calm nature as "not powerful enough"? What would change if you saw it as your greatest strength?
2. Who in your life has been soothed or calmed by your words? What did that moment teach you?
3. How comfortable are you with silence and pauses when you speak? What fears come up, and how might you work through them?
4. What belief about yourself needs to shift so that you can demonstrate your AIR energy more confidently?

Practical Tips

- **Pause Practice:** Record a short talk, then listen back and identify where you could have added pauses. Practice extending them by 2–3 seconds to let your words breathe.
- **Confidence Journal:** Write down one affirmation each day about your calm speaking style, e.g., *"My presence brings clarity and peace."* Over time, this builds belief.

- **Breath Alignment:** Practice speaking while following a slow breathing rhythm (inhale 4 counts, hold 2, exhale 6). This anchors pace and calm delivery.
- **Soft Power Rehearsal:** Practice delivering a key line both loudly and softly. Notice how the softer version often draws listeners in more effectively.
- **Silent Presence Exercise:** Before entering a room or starting a speech, stand in silence for 10 seconds. This builds comfort with presence and nonverbal authority.

Air in Action: Well-Known Examples

Susan Cain

Susan demonstrates AIR by leaning fully into her quiet nature. In her famous TED Talk, she believed in her message about the power of introverts and delivered it with gentleness and conviction. Her slower pace and thoughtful tone allowed her words to resonate worldwide.

Warren Buffett

Buffett speaks softly, with deliberate pacing that makes every word feel intentional. His calm tone soothes even in times of financial uncertainty. By believing in his quiet approach, he shows that confidence doesn't require volume, it requires clarity and presence.

Seth Godin

Known for his thoughtful presentations and blog-style delivery, Seth Godin demonstrates AIR by using simplicity and calm to cut through complexity. His slower pace and soft-spoken authority help listeners absorb his insights, proving that ideas land more powerfully when not rushed.

CHAPTER 18
Demonstrating Earth

To be persuasive, you must be believable and credible, which requires being truthful. - Edward R. Murrow.

Finally, let's talk about our natural persuaders. The best way to show off your gift of communication is to leverage your ability to persuade. And therefore, your first magic word is *convince*.

Always ensure that you believe in what you're saying before attempting to convince others. Lower your pitch and tone of voice. And don't use rising inflection in your statements unless you intentionally want to show doubt.

Demonstrate persuasion with confidence, share your message with conviction. It's one of your biggest strengths and superpowers.

The next magic word I have for you is *ground*. What does it mean? Ground yourself and ground your listeners. You are known for your ability to stand with both feet on the ground metaphorically. You aren't flying in the sky. You probably consider yourself a realist and take pride in it.

Most EARTH speakers I know possess incredible executive presence. When they speak, it feels like every statement falls heavily on the ground, with conviction and strength.

Embrace this ability of yours. Not only does it give you confidence and power, but it also helps the audience feel secure, comfortable, and at peace.

When we listen to someone who knows what they are talking about, it gives us a sense of contentment and security.

One of my best friends, whom I mentioned in earlier chapters, is a wonderful example of executive presence. That's one of the reasons people are drawn to her - there are too many uncertainties in the world. And when someone speaks with persuasion and presence, being grounded and not floating in the air with their ideas, it brings peace, and worries start to dissipate.

The third magic word for you is *emphasize*. Your speech is naturally emphatic. Tap into your passion and deliver a speech with strength and emphasis.

Use your natural pauses to make statements even more powerful. Trust your gut when it comes to choosing the right moment for a pause. Allow your listeners to chew and swallow your every thought. Help them digest your message so that it becomes a part of them.

If your speaking energy is EARTH, remember the following. With great power comes great responsibility. Don't take it lightly. If you have developed your style of speaking so much that it's natural for you to communicate with persuasion, your presentations are incredibly impactful. Be aware of your ability to change people's minds.

It's an amazing gift. Use it consciously with great awareness and humility.

Summary:

EARTH speakers demonstrate their power through persuasion, presence, and weight. When they *convince,* they do so with belief, confidence, and credibility. When they *ground,* they stand firm, creating security for themselves and their audience. And when they *emphasize,* they use pauses and deliberate delivery to make every word land with authority. Demonstrating Earth is about speaking with steady strength while remembering that this gift must be used with humility and responsibility.

Reflection Questions

1. Do you always believe in your own message before trying to persuade others? How might that affect your delivery?

2. How do people describe your presence when you speak: grounded, commanding, approachable?

3. What role do pauses currently play in your delivery? Do they strengthen or weaken your emphasis?

4. How do you ensure your persuasive ability is used responsibly, with humility and care for your audience?

Practical Tips

- **Conviction Test:** Before giving a talk, ask yourself: *Would I believe this message if I were in the audience?* Revise until the answer is yes.

- **Grounding Exercise:** Before stepping on stage, plant both feet firmly on the floor, breathe deeply, and visualize your energy moving downward. This stabilizes your presence.
- **Pause Power:** Mark 2–3 intentional pause points in your speech where emphasis is critical. Let silence underline the importance of your words.
- **Tone Awareness:** Practice lowering your pitch slightly on key statements to project authority and credibility.
- **Audience Trust Check:** After speaking, ask one or two listeners how your message made them feel. Did it build trust, clarity, or reassurance? Use their feedback to refine.

Earth in Action: Well-Known Examples

Angela Merkel

Merkel demonstrates Earth energy by grounding her leadership in calm, steady communication. Her deliberate tone and logical persuasion convinced audiences not through flash but through credibility and quiet strength.

Nelson Mandela

Mandela embodied conviction. Every word he spoke was rooted in belief and moral authority, which made his persuasion nearly unshakable. His pauses and emphasis allowed people to absorb not just his words but his values.

Brené Brown

Brené shows how Earth energy can blend authority with vulnerability. She convinces by sharing research and grounded truths, she establishes presence through authenticity, and she emphasizes key ideas with stories and pauses that stay with listeners.

CHAPTER 19
Speak With Emotional Intelligence

"When awareness is brought to an emotion, power is brought to your life." — Tara Meyer Robson

"What am I going to do? I can't remember what I have to say next."

My mind was starting to panic, almost ready to shut down. But that would've been a disaster. I knew it. A group of 40 young bankers was staring at me, waiting for the next part of their training to begin.

I could almost physically feel shame, fear, and anxiety creep through my body. And then my eyes stopped at the faces of young, brilliant professionals who were going to figure it out soon. So I had to pull myself together.

There was no time for panic. Suddenly, my brain switched to emergency mode, and the fog cleared, revealing everything like a blue sky on a gorgeous, sunny day.

I focused my attention on the listeners, put them in the center of my mind, rather than my troubles, and that's when I knew exactly what to say and do next.

This is a real story that happened a few years ago at a training I facilitated in NYC. When you look back at how I described it, you'll be able to see all four stages of Emotional Intelligence: Self-Awareness, Social Awareness, Self-Management, and Relationship Management.

Now, remember a moment during your presentation when you suddenly forgot what you wanted to say. What were your emotions? Describe them in as much detail as possible.

Ensure that you name emotions accurately and strive to understand their origins. That's Self Awareness.

As soon as you identify the emotions, you're equipped with enough information to start managing them. Pause, take a deep breath, and imagine that you're looking at yourself from the side. What do you see?

This objective view will help you cool down and get a new perspective. There's no Self-Management without Self-Awareness. First, take a moment to understand your state of mind and emotions. Then, you'll be able to take them under control.

While you're managing your own emotions, keep your eyes open for what's going on around you. How's your audience feeling? What's their reaction?

That's Social Awareness.

Develop the ability to read people's body language. Make it into your strengths. It may become one of your most essential skills as a speaker and a leader.

Another essential skill that will enhance your social awareness is Empathy. Your ability to understand people's emotions, more so to feel what they feel, will turn you into a superhuman. You'll know how to build relationships with anybody you want. And we all know there's no success in the world nowadays without good networking skills. Relationships are a crucial part of every aspect of our lives.

That brings us to the fourth stage of emotional intelligence: relationship management.

What do you think will help you the most in building and maintaining relationships? Surprisingly, it's not your speaking but your listening skills. Your ability to focus on another person, ask the right questions, and listen carefully to their answers with great and sincere care. Does that describe you? Remember the last conversation you had with someone. Was most of it about you, or did you show genuine interest in that person?

The most charismatic people with a high level of emotional intelligence are usually phenomenal listeners. They know how to show others they matter to them. These are the kind of people, when you're talking to them, suddenly you catch yourself thinking: "I've been talking non-stop about myself."

I sure hope you do catch yourself and don't just keep talking. Analyze your experience with such people. What do they do right? They make you feel comfortable and accepted. They listen with no judgment, truly caring about you and your story.

So, let's review. What are the four components of Emotional Intelligence? The best visual representation of them is in the following matrix.

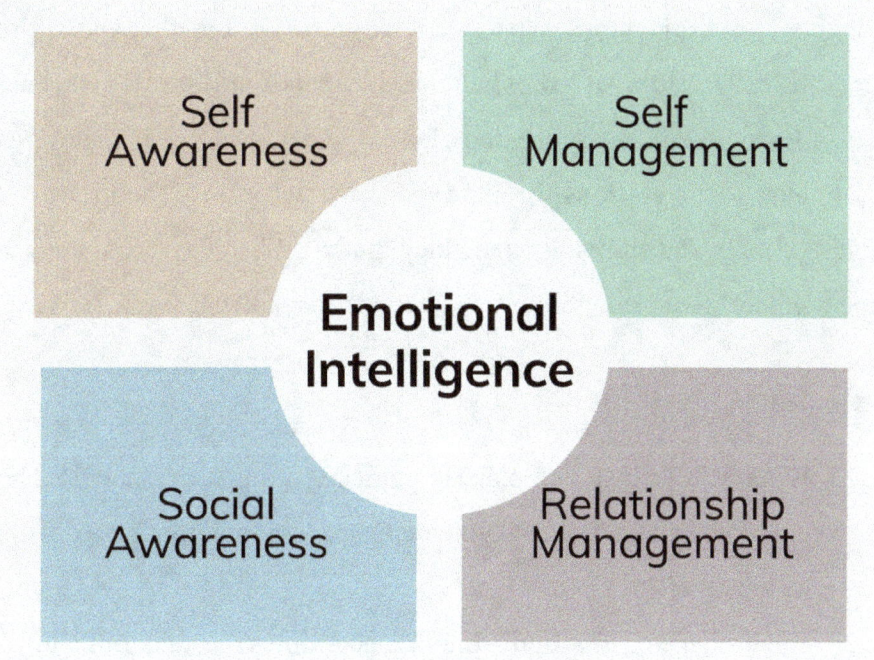

Summary:

Emotional Intelligence is the speaker's secret weapon. It begins with **self-awareness** — recognizing and naming emotions accurately. It grows through **self-management,** where we learn to pause, breathe, and redirect energy instead of letting it overwhelm us. It expands into **social awareness,** where we read the room, sense body language, and practice empathy. And it culminates in **relationship management,** where we build trust by listening deeply and showing others they matter. When these four elements come together, we speak with clarity, connection, and charisma.

Reflection Questions

1. When you've lost your place or panicked during a presentation, how did you handle it? Did you manage your emotions or did they manage you?
2. Which stage of Emotional Intelligence comes most naturally to you: awareness, management, empathy, or relationships? Which needs the most growth?
3. Think about the last time you listened deeply to someone. What did they feel in that moment? What did you learn?
4. How do you usually sense the emotions of your audience? What cues help you read the room best?
5. If your listeners were asked whether they felt truly "seen" by you, what would they say?

Practical Tips

- **Name It to Tame It:** In moments of stress, silently name the emotion you're feeling ("anxious," "impatient," "excited"). This reduces intensity and increases control.

- **The Pause Reset:** If nerves strike, pause and take one deep breath. This quick reset helps you re-enter with clarity instead of panic.

- **Empathy Rehearsal:** Before your next presentation, write down how your audience might be feeling about the topic. Then adjust your tone and examples to meet them there.

- **The 70/30 Listening Rule:** In conversations, aim to listen 70% of the time and speak 30%. It builds trust and deepens connections.

- **Mirror Awareness:** Practice noticing and subtly mirroring your audience's body language or tone. This strengthens rapport and shows understanding.

CHAPTER 20

Summary

It was the end of Day 2 of our training for bankers. Everyone was gathering their things and heading out the door to get a well-deserved rest.

"Can I ask you a question?" I heard a voice behind me. "Of course", I said

enthusiastically, turning around. A young woman was looking at me with sincere curiosity.

"How can you maintain the same level of energy for 7 hours straight? It's unbelievable!"

It was flattering to hear, but the answer was too easy to be impressive.

"I just love what I do. And every moment of it energizes me. I give my energy away, but I also receive a lot of it from all of you, from my audience."

As you can see, the secret to being full of energy lies in your passion for the topic and the people you're sharing it with.

Now, let's review everything we've discussed in this book so far.

There are four Speaking Energies: Fire, Water, Air, and Earth.

First, you DEFINED your Speaking Energy. You found what's most natural for you and what feels authentic. You defined your style of speaking.

Second, you DEVELOPED your Speaking Energy. You amplified your strengths and neutralized your weaknesses.

And finally, you DEMONSTRATE your amazing way of speaking, which shows the authentic you in your best light. Let yourself shine, owning your superpowers and showing them off to the world.

Remember that your power is comprised of Presence, Ownership, a Winner's mindset, Energy, and Resilience.

When your unique speaking energy comes to the front, your charisma shines. It allows you to show your most dominant type of Charisma (Focus, Visionary, Kindness, or Authority) and your best qualities as a speaker.

Unlock your speaking energy to unveil charisma and set your superpower free.

And finally, as an Emotionally Intelligent speaker, you possess high levels of Self-awareness, Social Awareness, Self-management, and Relationship Management.

Reflection Questions

1. Which speaking energy feels most natural to you and how have you embraced it since starting this book?
2. What's one strength you've amplified and one weakness you've learned to manage?
3. Where will you first demonstrate your speaking energy in the real world - in a meeting, a presentation, or a conversation?

4. How will you remind yourself to lead with Presence, Ownership, a Winner's Mindset, Energy, and Resilience?

Practical Next Steps

- **Choose One Action:** Don't try to apply everything at once. Pick one new technique or insight and practice it in your next speaking opportunity.
- **Keep an Energy Journal:** After every speech, presentation, or even important conversation, jot down: *What energy did I use? How did it feel? How did people respond?*
- **Ask for Feedback:** Invite a trusted friend or colleague to tell you how your energy comes across. Often others see strengths we don't.
- **Stretch into Other Energies:** Once you've mastered your dominant energy, experiment with borrowing a feature from another style, like Earth's pauses or Fire's passion.
- **Return Often:** Revisit these pages. Each time you grow as a speaker, you'll see new ways to apply these insights.

A Closing Encouragement

Remember: you don't need to become someone else to be a powerful speaker. Your energy - whether Fire, Water, Air, or Earth - is already enough. When you define it, develop it, and demonstrate it with Emotional Intelligence, you won't just speak. You'll inspire, persuade, and leave a mark.

Appendix - Exercises

FIRE

If you're like me, enthusiasm and passion burst out of you whenever you speak about something you love. That's when it's not easy for you to hold back emotions. However, it's important to be able to manage them. Here are a few exercises that will help you do that.

Calming exercises

1. Inhale, hold your breath for 3 seconds, exhale slowly. Repeat the process three times.
2. Relax all your muscles and begin feeling them, starting with your toes. Move up your body and consciously relax each muscle.
3. Breathe in slowly, counting to four and focusing on your breath. Breathe out, counting to four very slowly. Focus on your breath.

EQ Exercises

1. Develop self-awareness by practicing presence and mindfulness. For that, spend 1-3 minutes a day being mindful about your body or the food/drinks you intake. For example, feel your toes, your nose, move your toes, rub the tips of your fingers off each other. Drink coffee and think of nothing else but its taste and smell. Feel the breeze on your face.

2. Develop empathy by putting yourself into another person's shoes. Imagine what it would be like to feel what they feel. Allow yourself to experience the whole spectrum of emotions.

3. Manage your emotions by first recognizing when a feeling is too strong and is starting to overwhelm you. Pause, breathe, acknowledge the emotion, allow it to be present for a few seconds, and then release it.

WATER

Using Pauses

1. Practice using pauses when speaking without an audience. Maintain a pause longer than natural to become comfortable with it. When you get used to a longer pause in practice, in real life, you'll be using a natural, normal pause.

2. When pausing, establish eye contact. Let your audience feel your presence with them. It will engage them in your presentation. They'll become a part of it.

3. Substitute all your filler words, such as 'um', 'ah', 'so', 'you know', 'like', and others, with pauses. It will add a better flow to your speech and reduce the speed.

Vocal variety

1. Practice using various paces, rhythms, and pitches. Open a book on any page and start reading with one pitch and pace, then suddenly change it into another.

2. Recite tongue twisters. They'll help you focus on different sounds and practice emphasizing them. Recite them in alternating rhythms, pitches, and paces.

3. Practice good articulation and enunciation. You can use any text for that, as well as tongue twisters. Read sentences and intentionally enunciate the final sound of each word.

AIR

Vocal strength exercises

Lung strength and Breathing exercises

1. Inhale, then exhale while saying each letter of the alphabet, one at a time. For example, inhale, then exhale while saying 'A'. Inhale again and exhale while saying 'B'. Repeat the same process with as many letters as you can.

2. Go for a quick run, and while running, recite your speech. Or call a friend and make an effort to run and talk at the same time.

3. Open a book, inhale, and start reading a passage in one breath until all air is gone from your lungs. Inhale again and read the same passage, doing your best to let the air out gradually so that you're able to read a longer passage.

Projection

1. Hum the song "Happy birthday" with your mouth closed and lips sealed. When producing sound, make sure the air from your lungs

moves towards your closed lips, creating vibration. If your lips feel a little itchy because of the vibration, it means you're projecting your voice correctly. Practice until you do it right.

2. Imagine that you're standing in front of an audience of 100 people. You don't have a microphone, so you need to speak in a way that allows your voice to carry as far as possible. Now, open your mouth and say: "Hello and welcome!" Don't yell, just take it forward and project in front of you.

3. Keep your mouth closed and pretend you're yawning. Stretch your mouth as much as possible without opening it. It will make the muscles around your vocal cords more flexible and give you a wider range during speaking.

EARTH

Persuasion exercises

As you already know, focusing on your strengths and developing them will bring you much more success than working on your weaknesses. Being persuasive is a part of your nature. But if you don't develop this skill, it won't help you achieve your goals. Tools are useless if nobody puts them to work.

1. Practice using your low-pitched voice and falling inflection. Read a passage in a book, intentionally using your low pitch and bringing your intonation down at the end of every statement. Try using falling

tonality several times in a sentence in order to emphasize certain points.

2. Hone your skill by thinking up potential objections to your various beliefs and then handling those objections. Practice your convincing speech to prove your point in response to every objection. You can do it by yourself or with a friend/family member. Ask them to object to your statement and then overcome their objection.

3. Participate in debates. It could be a specialized debate club, an exercise you do with a group of friends, or even by yourself. All you need to do is choose a controversial statement, research the topic, collect arguments, and give a 5-minute speech proving your point.

Flow exercises

Having a tendency to be a grounded speaker who uses a lot of pauses might make your speeches seem heavy.

The following three exercises will help you lighten up and bring more flow to your speech.

1. Relax your articulation organs before a speech.
   a. Say me-mo several times, drastically moving your lips
   b. Open and close your mouth like a fish several times
   c. open your mouth and throat as if you're yawning.
2. When using pauses, make sure they are natural. Don't overdo them and don't just use them for effect. Read the room and sense the audience's reaction to your pause.

3. Add flow to your speech. For practice, start by listening to music to get into a melodic rhythm. Then, rehearse your presentation, imagining that you're singing a song and all your words are connected by a melody.

Connect with Natasha:

https://natashabazilevych.com/

https://www.linkedin.com/in/natashabazilevych/

https://www.facebook.com/nbazilevich/

https://www.instagram.com/natbazilevych/

Speak With Power Podcast on all main platforms.